DWIGHT 

SUCCESS

— HAS —

RECEIPTS

PROVEN STRATEGIES AND TANGIBLE TOOLS FOR ACHIEVING SUCCESS

Publishing support provided by Pen and Parchment Publishing LLC
15127 Main ST E Sumner, WA 98390

Hardcover ISBN: 979-8-9886156-0-6
Paperback ISBN: 979-8-9886156-1-3
Digital ISBN: 979-8-9886156-2-0

For booking, permissions, inquiries, or bulk purchases, please contact:

Pen and Parchment Publishing LLC
15127 Main St E Sumner, WA 98390
PenandParchmentPublishing@gmail.com
PenandParchmentPublishing.net

Because of the dynamic nature of the Internet, web addresses or links contained in this book may have been changed since publication and may no longer be valid. The content of this book and all expressed opinions are those of the author and do not reflect the publisher or the publishing team. The author is solely responsible for all content included herein.

Library of Congress Control Number:

Cover design by Velma Alex

Edited by Sam Wright

Photograph by Jewel Casimire-Fleary

Printed in the United States of America

FIRST EDITION

"To my wife Chanelle,

As we celebrate over two decades of shared moments, challenges, and joys, I wanted to take a moment to express my gratitude. Your unwavering support, love, and partnership have been the foundation of my journey, and I couldn't have asked for a more incredible companion by my side.

This book, *"Success Has Receipts,"* is not just a collection of words on pages—it's a reflection of the countless lessons we've learned, the triumphs we've celebrated, and the growth we've experienced together. Your presence has been the driving force behind my aspirations and the inspiration behind every endeavor.

Thank you for standing with me through thick and thin, for believing in my dreams, and for sharing your own aspirations with me. This book is a tribute to the beautiful life we've built together and a testament to the remarkable person you are.

Here's to the next chapter of our journey—may it be filled with even more success, love, and cherished memories.

Love,
[Dwight]"

"To Deshawn, Jada, Jewel, and Michael,

May the pages of this book reflect the dreams I hold for each of you. May it inspire your growth, guide your paths, and remind you that success is not just measured in achievements, but in the impact, you make on the world. You are my greatest accomplishments, and I dedicate this book to the legacy you will create.

With all my love,
[Dad]"

MESSAGE FROM THE AUTHOR

This book is dedicated to all those striving for success in their personal and professional lives. To those who have faced obstacles and setbacks but refused to give up on their dreams. To those who are determined to create a better future for themselves and their loved ones. I wrote this book to inspire you, encourage you, and provide you with the tools and mindset needed to achieve the success you desire. Remember, success is not a destination but a journey. It is more of an internal fulfilment than external measures. Keep moving forward and never give up.

TABLE OF CONTENT

INTRODUCTION

"Do not go where the path may lead, go instead where there is no path and leave a trail." - Ralph Waldo Emerson

In this book, we will explore the concept of success and what it means to pursue it. We will delve into the ways success is perceived and measured, and we will provide practical advice on how to achieve it. Success is not a one-size-fits-all concept, and what works for one person may not work for another. However, by understanding the fundamental principles of success and applying them to our unique situations, we can all achieve our goals and live fulfilling lives.

WHAT IS SUCCESS?

Success can mean different things to different people. For some, it may mean financial prosperity, while for others, it may mean achieving personal goals or making a positive impact in the world. Regardless of how you define success, one thing is certain: it requires hard work, dedication, and a willingness to learn and grow.

Success is a universal concept that has intrigued people for centuries. It is a term that is used frequently in our society, yet its meaning can vary widely depending on who you ask. Some may define success as achieving wealth or fame, while others may view it in terms of personal fulfillment or happiness. Regardless of how it is defined, success remains a fundamental goal that many strive to attain.

Another essential element of success is the ability to measure it. Measuring success allows us to track our progress, identify areas we need to improve, and stay motivated. However, measuring success can be challenging because success is often subjective and elusive. It is essential to develop a clear understanding of what success means to us and identify metrics to measure our progress.

Getting to success requires self-reflection, perseverance, and willingness to take risks and learn from failure. It is not a destination overnight but a continuous process of growth and development. By understanding what success means to us and developing a clear plan to achieve it, we can overcome obstacles and setbacks and continue to move toward our goals.

As humans, it's natural to compare ourselves to others. We look at our peers, colleagues, and even strangers on social media and wonder why we haven't achieved the same success. However, constantly comparing ourselves to others can harm our mental health and overall well-being.

First, it's important to understand that everyone's journey is unique. We all have different backgrounds, experiences, and circumstances shaping our lives and paths. Comparing ourselves to others ignores these factors and creates an unrealistic standard to live up to. It's unfair to ourselves to hold ourselves to someone else's standards because we are not them.

Second, success is subjective and multifaceted. Success means different things to different people, and it's not limited to just material possessions or achievements. Some people value close relationships, personal growth, or positively impacting their community, while others may prioritize financial stability or career advancement. Comparing ourselves to others based on one aspect of success ignores the other areas where we may excel.

Comparing ourselves to others can lead to inadequacy, jealousy, or resentment. When we focus on what others have achieved, we lose sight of our accomplishments and progress. Celebrating our successes and recognizing that they are as valid and meaningful as anyone else's is important.

Instead of comparing ourselves to others, we should focus on our journeys and progress. We should set our goals based on our values and priorities and work toward achieving them at our own pace. Remember that success is not a destination but a journey; there will always be ups and downs. We can live a more fulfilling and authentic life by focusing on our growth and progress.

Each chapter will include real-life examples, exercises, and tools to help you apply the concepts to your life. By the end of this book, you'll have a roadmap for achieving success tailored to your unique strengths, interests, and goals.

So, whether you're starting out on your journey or looking to take your success to the next level, let's dive in and explore the recipes for success!

Practical Exercise: Define Your Personal Vision of Success

Instructions: Take time to reflect and write down your vision of success. Consider various areas of your life, such as career, relationships, health, and development. What does success mean to you in each area? Be specific and paint a vivid picture of what success looks like for you

CHAPTER ONE
UNDERSTANDING THE CONCEPT OF SUCCESS

"Success is not the key to happiness. Happiness is the key to success. If you love what you are doing, you will be successful." - Albert Schweitzer

Success is not an accident; it requires careful planning and goal setting. This chapter will discuss the importance of setting clear goals and creating a plan to achieve them. We will also explore strategies to help you stay on track and achieve your goals.

Despite the subjective nature of success, it is an important concept to pursue. Pursuing success can bring satisfaction, fulfillment, and a sense of purpose to our lives. It can motivate us to work hard, take risks, and push ourselves beyond our limits. Success can also bring tangible rewards, such as financial stability, recognition, and personal growth.

However, pursuing success can also be challenging. It requires dedication, hard work, and perseverance. Success is not always guaranteed, and setbacks and failures are inevitable. Nevertheless, pursuing success can be rewarding and fulfilling, ultimately leading to a better life.

Success starts with a clear vision of what you want to achieve. Without a goal, you're wandering aimlessly and hoping for the best. However, setting a goal is not enough. You also need a plan to achieve it. According to the philosopher Aristotle, success results from living a virtuous life. He believed that success was not solely based on external factors such as wealth or power but on internal factors such as character and moral excellence. Similarly, psychologist Abraham Maslow argued that success is achieved through self-actualization or the realization of one's full potential.

THE IMPORTANCE OF PURSUING SUCCESS

Pursuing success can have a positive impact on individuals, relationships, and communities. Success can increase self-esteem, confidence, and motivation, leading to greater personal fulfillment and happiness. It can also provide financial stability and security, improving overall quality of life.

In addition to personal benefits, success can have a positive impact on relationships. Successful individuals may have more opportunities to build meaningful connections with others, and their achievements can inspire and motivate those around them. Success can lead to positive contributions to society, such as creating jobs, advancing scientific research, or promoting social justice.

DIFFERENT PERCEPTIONS OF SUCCESS AMONG INDIVIDUALS

Various factors, including culture, upbringing, and personal values shape individuals' perceptions of success. For example, in some cultures, success may be defined by achieving a high level of education or securing a prestigious job, while in others, success may be measured by having a large family and community involvement. Upbringing can also play a role in shaping one's perception of success. Children raised in families that prioritize academic achievement may place a greater emphasis on education as a measure of success, while those from families that value creativity and artistic expression may view success in terms of pursuing their passions.

Personal values can also influence how individuals define success. Some people prioritize financial stability and career advancement, while others prioritize personal relationships and emotional well-being. These individual differences can lead to varying perceptions of success and different paths to achieving it.

In F. Scott Fitzgerald's The Great Gatsby, the character Jay Gatsby is driven by his desire for success and societal recognition. His pursuit of wealth and status ultimately leads to his downfall, highlighting the dangers of valuing external measures of success over internal fulfillment. A book worth reading.

In Ralph Waldo Emerson's essay "Self-Reliance," he argues that success is achieved by trusting oneself and following one's path rather than conforming to societal norms or expectations. He emphasizes the importance of self-discovery and individuality in achieving true success.

Another literary reference to success is Malcolm Gladwell's Outliers, which explores the factors contributing to success. Gladwell argues that success is not solely based on individual talent or hard work but also external factors such as culture, family background, and opportunities.

He suggests that success is often a result of these factors rather than individual merit alone.

Whether we believe it is by our own merits or external means, it is our responsibility to reflect on our values and goals and strive toward a version of success that aligns with our beliefs and aspirations. Ultimately, success is not a destination but a journey, and it is up to each individual to define and pursue their path toward fulfillment and happiness.

In addition, success can be defined in many ways, and its meaning can vary widely depending on individual perspectives and circumstances. Pursuing success can positively impact individuals, relationships, and communities, but it is essential to prioritize personal fulfillment and happiness over external measures of success. Culture, upbringing, and personal values shape one's perception of success, and it is important to recognize and respect these individual differences.

TANGIBLE TOOLS AND STRATEGIES

GOAL SETTING: Set clear and specific goals that align with your values and aspirations. Use the SMART (Specific, Measurable, Achievable, Relevant, Time-bound) framework to create well-defined goals that provide focus and direction.

ACTION PLANNING: Break down your goals into actionable steps. Create a detailed plan that outlines the specific tasks, milestones, and timelines needed to achieve your objectives. This will help you stay organized and track your progress.

Time Management: Develop effective time management skills by prioritizing tasks, setting deadlines, and eliminating distractions. Use productivity tools such as calendars, to-do lists, and time-tracking apps to optimize your time and ensure efficient use of your resources.

CONTINUOUS LEARNING: Commit to lifelong learning and personal development. Stay updated with industry trends, seek new knowledge and skills, and invest in self-improvement through books, courses, workshops, or mentorship programs. Expanding your knowledge and skills will enhance your competence and increase your chances of success.

NETWORKING AND RELATIONSHIP BUILDING: Cultivate a strong professional network by connecting with like-minded individuals, industry experts, and mentors. Attend networking events, join professional associations, and leverage online platforms to establish meaningful relationships. Building a supportive network can provide valuable opportunities, collaborations, and guidance on your journey to success.

RESILIENCE AND ADAPTABILITY: Develop resilience to overcome setbacks and challenges. Embrace failure as a learning experience, maintain a positive mindset, and practice adaptability in changing circumstances. Resilience allows you to bounce back stronger and find alternative solutions when obstacles arise.

Self-Care and Well-being: Prioritize self-care and maintain a healthy work-life balance. Take care of your physical and mental well-being by incorporating regular exercise, adequate rest, healthy eating habits, and stress management techniques into your routine. Taking care of yourself enhances your energy, focus, and overall productivity.

ACCOUNTABILITY AND TRACKING PROGRESS: Hold yourself accountable for your actions and progress toward your goals. Regularly review your achievements, assess your strengths and areas for improvement, and make necessary adjustments to stay on track. Consider using accountability tools such as journaling, progress-tracking apps, or accountability partners to help you stay focused and motivated.

Remember, these tools provide practical strategies, but their effectiveness depends on your commitment, perseverance, and adaptability. Success is a personal journey, and finding the right tools that work for you may require experimentation and adjustment.

CHAPTER TWO
THE MINDSET OF SUCCESS

"Whether you think you can, or you think you can't—you're right."
- Henry Ford

A success-oriented mindset plays a crucial role in achieving one's goals and realizing their fullest potential. It encompasses a set of attitudes, beliefs, and mental frameworks that empower individuals to overcome challenges, persist in the face of obstacles, and maintain a positive outlook on their journey toward success.

IMPORTANCE OF A SUCCESS-ORIENTED MINDSET

A success-oriented mindset is vital because it shapes how individuals approach their goals and navigate the inevitable ups and downs. A mindset focused on success cultivates resilience, determination, and self-belief. It instills the belief that obstacles are merely growth opportunities, and that failure is a stepping stone toward ultimate achievement.

GOAL-SETTING AND ITS SIGNIFICANCE IN ACHIEVING SUCCESS

An essential aspect of the success mindset is the practice of goal setting. Setting clear, specific, and meaningful goals provides a roadmap for success. Goals serve as guideposts that help individuals stay focused, motivated, and aligned with their desired outcomes. By defining objectives and breaking them down into actionable steps, individuals can better track their progress and make the adjustments to move forward.

POSITIVE THINKING AND ATTITUDE

Positive thinking is a key component of the success mindset. It involves maintaining an optimistic outlook, focusing on possibilities rather than limitations, and reframing challenges as opportunities. Positive thinking helps individuals develop a solution-oriented mindset, enabling them to overcome obstacles with creativity and resourcefulness. By cultivating positive thoughts and attitudes, individuals can effectively manage stress, boost self-confidence, and maintain the resilience needed to persevere in adversity.

RESILIENCE AND DETERMINATION

Resilience is a vital quality in the mindset of success. It refers to the ability to bounce back from setbacks, adapt to change, and maintain focus despite challenges. Resilient individuals see failures as temporary setbacks, learning opportunities, and necessary steps for success. They embrace the belief that with every failure comes a lesson, and they are determined to apply those lessons to improve and progress further.

SELF-DISCIPLINE AND SELF-MOTIVATION

Self-discipline and self-motivation are essential pillars of the success mindset. Self-discipline involves the ability to make consistent and purposeful actions aligned with one's goals, even when faced with distractions or temptations. Self-motivation drives individuals to stay committed, persevere, and maintain their focus on long-term objectives.

Cultivating self-discipline and self-motivation often requires setting clear priorities, managing time effectively, and fostering a strong sense of purpose and intrinsic motivation.

DEVELOPING A SUCCESS-ORIENTED MINDSET

Developing a success-oriented mindset is a lifelong journey that requires self-reflection, conscious effort, and continuous growth. Some strategies to nurture and strengthen this mindset include:

Self-awareness: Gain clarity about your values, strengths, and areas for improvement. Understand how your beliefs and thought patterns impact your actions and outcomes.

Positive affirmations and visualization: Practice positive self-talk and visualize your success. Create affirmations that reinforce your confidence and belief in your abilities.

Surrounding yourself with positive influences: Seek supportive and like-minded individuals who inspire and motivate you. Engage in communities or networks that foster a success mindset.

Continuous learning and personal development: Embrace a growth mindset by seeking opportunities for learning, skill development, and self-improvement. Read books, attend workshops, and seek mentorship to expand your knowledge and skills.

Gratitude and mindfulness: Cultivate gratitude for the present moment and the progress you have made. Practice mindfulness to stay focused on the present and avoid being overwhelmed by future challenges.

A success-oriented mindset lays the foundation for achieving goals and fulfilling one's potential. By adopting a success-oriented mindset, individuals can overcome obstacles, stay motivated, and maintain a positive outlook throughout their journey. It requires consistent effort and self-reflection to cultivate and strengthen this mindset.

TOOLS AND PRACTICES TO INCORPORATE ON YOUR SUCCESS JOURNEY.

Affirmations: Use positive affirmations to reprogram your thoughts and beliefs. Create statements that reflect the mindset of success and repeat them daily. For example, "I am capable of achieving my goals," "I embrace challenges as opportunities for growth," or "I deserve success." Repeat these affirmations aloud or write them down to reinforce positive thinking patterns.

Visualization: Practice visualization techniques to mentally rehearse your success. Close your eyes and vividly imagine yourself achieving your goals, overcoming challenges, and experiencing the emotions associated with success. Visualization helps strengthen your belief in your abilities and aligns your actions with your desired outcomes.

Gratitude Journaling: Keep a gratitude journal where you regularly write down things you are grateful for. Cultivating gratitude helps shift your focus to the positive aspects of your life and fosters a mindset of abundance. Each day, list at least three things you are grateful for, including progress, achievements, support, or lessons learned.

Goal Setting Tools: Utilize goal-setting tools to support your success mindset. Use a journal or a digital tool to set specific, measurable, achievable, relevant, and time-bound (SMART) goals. Break down larger goals into smaller, actionable steps and track your progress. This helps maintain focus, provides clarity, and allows for a sense of accomplishment along the way.

Daily Reflection and Journaling: Set aside time each day for self-reflection and journaling. Reflect on your successes, challenges, and lessons learned. Write down your thoughts, emotions, and observations. This practice encourages self-awareness, helps identify patterns, and fosters continuous personal growth.

Accountability Systems: Establish accountability systems to stay on track and maintain motivation. Find an accountability partner or join a mastermind group where you can share your goals, progress, and challenges. Regular check-ins and discussions with others focused on success can provide support, encouragement, and valuable insights.

Mindfulness and Meditation: Incorporate mindfulness and meditation practices into your routine. These techniques help you stay present, reduce stress, and cultivate a calm and focused mindset. Regular mindfulness exercises or guided meditation sessions enhance self-awareness, mental clarity, and emotional well-being.

Continuous Learning: Develop a habit of continuous learning to expand your knowledge and skills. Read books, listen to podcasts, take online courses, or attend seminars related to your field of interest or personal development. Lifelong learning keeps your mind open, sharp, and adaptable, empowering you to stay ahead and seize opportunities.

Remember, these tools support and reinforce the mindset of success. Experiment with different techniques, choose the ones that resonate with you, and incorporate them into your daily routine. Consistency and dedication to these practices will help strengthen your success mindset and propel you toward achieving your goals.

Finally, it's important to celebrate your successes along the way. Achieving success is a journey, not a destination, and it's important to acknowledge and celebrate the progress you make along the way. By reflecting on your accomplishments and celebrating your victories, you can stay motivated and inspired as you continue to work toward your goals. Remember, success is not a one-time event but a continuous journey of growth and improvement.

Practical Exercise: Reframe Limiting Beliefs
Instructions: Identify a limiting belief that may hold you back from achieving success. Write it down and then challenge it by finding evidence to the contrary. Reframe the belief into a more empowering and supportive statement. Practice repeating this new belief daily to reinforce a positive mindset.

CHAPTER THREE

THE POWER OF PLANNING AND EXECUTION

"Success is the sum of small efforts, repeated day in and day out." -Robert Collier

Planning and execution are critical components of achieving success. While goals provide direction, the deliberate planning and consistent execution of actionable steps turn aspirations into reality. Let's explore why planning and execution are essential and how they contribute to achieving success.

THE ROLE OF PLANNING AND EXECUTION IN ACHIEVING SUCCESS

Planning serves as the roadmap that guides individuals toward their desired outcomes. It involves setting clear objectives, defining strategies, and outlining the specific actions required to accomplish those objectives. Planning allows for a structured approach, helps anticipate potential challenges, and maximizes the efficient use of resources.

Execution is the implementation of the plan—the actual action taken to move closer to the desired goals. Without execution, even the most well-crafted plans remain mere ideas. Execution involves taking consistent and focused action, overcoming obstacles, and staying committed to the plan in the face of challenges and distractions.

CREATING A PLAN FOR SUCCESS

Creating a comprehensive plan involves several key steps. First, clearly define your objectives and identify what success means to you. Next, break down your goals into smaller, actionable tasks that are manageable and measurable. Consider setting milestones and deadlines to track progress and maintain momentum.

Additionally, identify the resources, skills, and knowledge required to achieve your goals. Assess any potential obstacles or risks that may arise along the way and develop contingency plans to address them. Remember, flexibility is essential in planning as circumstances may change, and adjustments may be necessary.

BREAKING DOWN GOALS INTO MANAGEABLE STEPS

Breaking down larger goals into smaller, manageable steps is a powerful strategy that promotes clarity and progress. When goals are broken down, they become less overwhelming and more actionable. Each step becomes a mini goal, making it easier to focus, track progress, and celebrate achievements along the way.

Consider using tools such as a task management app or project management software to create a visual representation of your goals and tasks. These tools provide a clear overview of your progress, enable you to prioritize tasks, and set reminders for important deadlines.

TAKING ACTION TOWARD GOALS

Execution is where plans come to life. Taking consistent action is crucial for making progress and achieving success. It requires discipline, focus, and a commitment to follow through with the tasks identified in your plan.

Developing a habit of daily or weekly action toward your goals is key. Break down your tasks further into smaller, actionable steps that can be accomplished within a specific timeframe. Prioritize your tasks based on their importance and urgency and consciously allocate dedicated time for working on them.

Use productivity tools such as time-tracking apps, Pomodoro timers, or habit trackers to help you manage your time effectively and stay focused. These tools can assist in breaking down your work into manageable chunks, boost productivity, and maintain accountability.

THE IMPORTANCE OF CONSISTENCY

Consistency is a vital ingredient in the recipe for success. It involves showing up consistently, following through with your plans, and persisting even when faced with challenges or setbacks. Consistency builds momentum and establishes a positive habit loop that fuels progress.

To cultivate consistency, develop a routine that supports your goals. Set aside specific time slots dedicated to working on your tasks each day or week. Create a conducive environment that minimizes distractions and maximizes focus. Surround yourself with supportive individuals who can hold you accountable and provide encouragement along the way.

TOOLS FOR SUCCESS:

Gantt Charts: Gantt charts are visual planning tools that help schedule and track tasks. They provide a clear timeline view of your project, highlighting task dependencies and deadlines. Gantt charts enable you to manage your tasks, allocate resources effectively, and track progress, making them valuable tools for success.

TO-DO LISTS

To-do lists are simple yet effective tools for organizing and prioritizing tasks. They help you stay focused and ensure that important actions are not overlooked. Break down your goals into actionable items and create daily or weekly to-do lists. Update and review your lists regularly to stay on track and maintain productivity.

TIME MANAGEMENT TECHNIQUES

Time management techniques, such as the Pomodoro Technique or Time Blocking, can enhance your productivity and focus. The Pomodoro Technique involves working in focused sprints with short breaks, while Time Blocking involves allocating specific time slots for different tasks or activities. Experiment with different techniques and find the one that works best for you.

PROJECT MANAGEMENT SOFTWARE

Project management software, such as Trello, Asana, or Monday.com, can be valuable tools for planning and executing your goals. These platforms allow you to create and track tasks, set deadlines, collaborate with others, and visualize your progress. They provide a centralized space to manage your projects and keep all relevant information in one place.

ACCOUNTABILITY PARTNERS OR GROUPS

Find an accountability partner or join a mastermind group to enhance your commitment and motivation. An accountability partner shares their goals with you, and you both hold each other accountable for acting. A mastermind group consists of individuals who meet regularly to provide support, guidance, and feedback. Engaging with like-minded individuals can boost your accountability and provide valuable insights.

JOURNALING

Journaling is a powerful tool for self-reflection, goal tracking, and mindset development. Use a journal to record your thoughts, track your progress, and reflect on your successes and challenges. Regularly reviewing your journal can provide insights into your growth, help identify patterns, and serve as a source of motivation.

Remember, these tools support your planning and execution process. Experiment with different tools and techniques to find what works best for you. The key is finding a system that keeps you organized, motivated, and on track to achieve your goals. Combine the power of planning and execution with the appropriate tools, and you'll be well-equipped to embark on your journey to success.

PRACTICAL EXERCISE

GOAL SETTING AND ACTION PLANNING INSTRUCTIONS

Set a specific and measurable goal you want to achieve. Break down the goal into smaller, actionable steps. Use the Goal-Setting Worksheet (Example Worksheet 1) to write down your goal and the steps required. Assign deadlines to each step and track your progress regularly.

Now Let's Hear From J. White And See How He Was Able To Succeed By Learning From Failure, How He And His Partner Aim To Be Succeed By Growing Their Business, And How They Also Touch on the Idea of Success being a continuous Journey with different levels of accomplishment to achieve over time:

https://www.richgirlsmuseum.com/
https://www.carolinashyt.com/

J. White and Marteekia Entrepreneurs - Courtesy of J. White

J. White with Mark Cuban - Courtesy of J. White

J. White All Business - Courtesy of J. White

J. White in Carolina Shyt - Courtesy of J. White

Dwight: Yeah, man, everything is good. I was just on my way home; traffic was kind of heavy coming from work. I'm over in Washington State now.

J. White: Oh yeah, Washington. Okay.

Dwight: Yeah, I'm up here now. So what do you go by now, 42 Love? J White?

J. White: Nah, you know what? I love that name, 42 Love, because it sticks with you. See how you know that now? I probably haven't even said that sh*t in three months, but my girl is hating on that name. But that should just be my name; 42 Love is a tough ass name.

Dwight: It is.

J. White: Yeah, I'm 42. But nah, I'm J. White, though, so yeah. I'm going to be 42.

Dwight: I'm feeling it. I'm feeling it. I'm feeling it. Well, the last and first time I saw you was in LA at that time.

J. White: At that conference, right?

Dwight: Yeah, the conference.

J. White: Yeah. Dwight: We met at that conference in, was it '18? 2018? I think it was '18.

J. White: I can't remember. Yeah, we linked up at the conference. Been cool ever since.

Dwight: Yep. I think it was, yeah, 2018. Something around there

J. White: It's crazy because I lost my Instagram page for like three years.

Dwight: Dang.

J White: I lost my Instagram page from '20 to '23. I just got it back a few months ago because I don't know if you followed my Carolina [01:53 inaudible] page.

Dwight: Yeah, I do.

J. White: Oh, okay. Yeah, I had this page, and then I was embracing some pictures, and I didn't know they'd asked me to verify that it was me, and they were asking to, like they told me they were texting the old phone number that I didn't have any more. And then the other choice was an email address that I didn't have any more. So they were like, basically, they couldn't get in contact with me, so they had my page just on hold for three years. And then one day out of nowhere, I woke up like, Man, I'm going to get back into my page. And I logged in, and it worked, and I was like, what?

Dwight: Yeah. Because I remember you posting all the comedy skit stuff.

J. White: Yeah.

Dwight: And then I didn't see it for a while, but yeah, man, that's good stuff. It's crazy because I met a lot of people at that conference too. And some people I kept in contact with made some great business and stuff out of it.

J. White: I'm going to set my phone right here for now because it was a big lightning storm. It just came down. I don't want to hold my phone.

Dwight: Yep. Exactly. J. White: What's the word, though?

Dwight: Yeah, man. So, I'm getting ready to drop this book, so I'm putting a couple of success stories, like yours and my brother-in-law, who got a couple clubs upstate New York and a little Toro business he was doing out in Hawaii, and then trying to get another female business owner in their fashion that does fashion. So, I'm just trying to get stories of success through the ups and downs, and the title of the book, as you see, is Success Has Receipts.

J. White: Yes, sir.

Dwight: Yeah, so definitely. We know there are ups and downs.

J. White: You said the title of the book is Receipts.

Dwight: Success Has Receipts.

J. White: Oh, okay. What does that title mean to you?

Dwight: So, for me, when I started writing and trying to get titles for the book, I also listened to a lot of podcasts and stuff on businesses, real estate, and things like that. And the idea came to me: Success has receipts because success does have receipts. You go through the ups and downs, the failures, and the struggles; you write out your goals; you want to make a plan for whatever you want to do. And you come from, you know, your personal story and whatever that experience is. And through success, you get receipts; you get the fruit of your labor. You work through those ups and downs, and you get to that destination, that point. And some people don't make it. Some people don't make it to that destination even though they put forth their effort on that journey. But some people don't stick with it, and you just have to stick with it through thick and thin. And you end up right where you want to be, and you end up right where you want to be. You put forth the effort and the time. You've got to put forward that time and that effort, and out comes that receipt because you put in perseverance, and perseverance is a cost. Whatever it is, you put that time and that cost in because you had to pay for this and that. You had to do your research, market research, and all that stuff, so you put in that time, and all those things that you put into your business, those receipts came. So punch that $50,000, that $20,000, and that $10,000 into perseverance, into failure, whatever it may be, and out comes that receipt. And you get through on that other end; whatever that obstacle is, you get over it and out spit the receipts of success. If you can, tell me who J. White is.

J White: J White is a 40-year-old man. I'm actually 42 now. Born in Queens, New York. I moved to Greensboro, North Carolina, when I was nine. I'm just an entrepreneur trying to find a play.

Dwight: I'm originally from Brooklyn, so that hustle mentality is definitely there.

J. White: Oh yeah.

J. White: Traffic is like crazy right here.

Dwight: Yeah. So originally from Queens, Greensboro, North Carolina. Did your childhood, your values, and your morals play a part in your success?

J. White: Yeah, I think so. I think I grew up in a big family. I remember when I got my first job, I didn't like the manager, and my grandma told me that I didn't have to work anywhere, but I didn't like the manager. She said, You can quit that job and start your own business.

Dwight: So she instilled that drive in you?

J. White: Yeah, I would say that.

Dwight: Okay. Did your mom play a big role in that as well?

J. White: My mom was always working. She wasn't around a lot. I was a badass kid in school, so if my mom instilled anything in me, I don't think she was a part of my entrepreneurial hustle.

Dwight: And congratulations, by the way, on your wedding.

J. White: I appreciate it.

Dwight: Definitely, definitely.

J. White: Yeah. But like I was saying, it was probably more so my grandma who instilled the idea of being an entrepreneur.

Dwight: Okay. So, a lot of people don't see; they see the bright lights and the success, but they don't see what happens behind the scenes. What you've got to do, what it takes, the effort, the pain, the long flights, the road trips—whatever you've got to do to get what you need done.

J. White: What were you saying?

Dwight: Yeah. So, I say people see the fruits, they see the success, they see the bright lights, but they don't see what goes on behind the scenes—the long trips, the road trips, the flights, the long flights, the capital you've got to put in to make your goals a reality. They don't see that. They think it's an overnight thing, but it's not. So, what does success mean to you personally?

J. White: Success is having the freedom to do what you want to do in life while still having the discipline to do what you need to do. I have three businesses right now. I got my Carolina Big Clothing Line, Underground Rich Studios, and Rich Girls Museum, which all have success that allows me to just work on being creative. I don't have to go out and find another job working for somebody else, but I'm not exactly where I want to be in all three of those businesses. You know what I'm saying? But I am allowed freedom and a somewhat luxurious lifestyle.

Dwight: That first sentence you say is definitely a quote for success. And out of that comes the receipt of success and how much work you put in. Because if you don't put in any work into it, you don't get the results—the results of those receipts—it ain't going to spit out nothing for you.

J. White: No, for sure

Dwight: So how do you measure success in your life?

J. White: How do I measure success? I measure success with freedom. Freedom to do whatever you want. The more you can do whatever you want, the more successful I feel like you are. For me, like I said, I have three businesses, and all three of them pay for their sales. So, I could literally wake up or sleep in the bed all day and those businesses work for me overnight, or now me and my wife have been taking meetings on how to grow the business. I think they're multimillion dollar businesses on paper, but in the cash, we don't have multimillion dollars from the business, but they all have the potential to be that. But me and my lady love to party. We like to hang out and just be free. So, since our businesses work for ourselves and we don't really have to think about making money, we like to party a lot, but now we've got these new goals that we're trying to hit. You know what I'm saying? New cars that we want to buy. And we got a lot of opportunities through the businesses that we created. So right now, we focus on really growing them into high volumes.

Dwight: Okay. So, the businesses—the three businesses—do you own the property that it sits on?

J. White: No, they're all in the same vicinity. I ain't going to lie; that's a problem too. You know what I'm saying? Like, just moving on because, I mean, I was born a hustler, you know what I'm saying? I come from the streets, and I don't have an education. I dropped out of high school, and I started hustling from there. I stumbled across these businesses while managing my cousin, who does music. And we were spending so much money on music studios that he ended up quitting music and telling me that I should do music because it's my passion. I tried it, and then I got tired of paying for studios, so I bought a studio and just realized that it's a better business for me to be not doing music, just putting artists in the studio, and then the Rich Girls Museum was a business idea that me and Marteekia came up with together. And then Carolina [20:10 inaudible] was just something—a clothing line that I made up because I was living in LA and I wanted everybody to know I was from North Carolina. So just having these businesses, like a music studio in North Carolina, makes a lot of people want to smoke weed. But in North Carolina, weed is illegal. And then you've got church people or just a different culture of people that live next door to me at the studio who don't like weed. So when they smell it, they go to the landlord and say, Oh, it's smelling like weed next door. Then the landlord came and threatened me, saying, Hey, your neighbors keep saying they smell weed; we're going to have to kick you out. So then I say, Okay, boom, my neighbors end up moving, and then I get the building next door to the studio so we can smoke weed. I don't smoke, but my clientele can smoke weed. And now that we have that building, they can smoke weed, but now we don't know what to call this building. We just got a building just so they could smoke weed. But then we came up with this Rich Girls Museum idea from selling women's clothes, and then we ended up putting that next door. So now we have a whole business next door that made a million dollars in the first year. The only reason we got the building was because we needed it so another neighbor couldn't move in and complain about the weed smoke.

Dwight: So it worked out.

J. White: Yeah. It worked itself out.

Dwight: Yeah. It worked itself out.

J. White: So recently I had a shooting at the studio. I had a guy that was in there recording, and he had some problems with some guys, and they knew he was in there recording. And when he was leaving the studio, they shot up my studio. So that was like one of the first things

I learned about not having my own land and having my business on my land because my landlord told me or the property manager told me he doesn't give a damn how long I've been there. I've been there for 12 years, but he told me he doesn't give a damn how long I've been there, and he doesn't care how much I invested in my business. He'll tear it up and turn it back into an office building, and he'll rent it out to somebody who's not going to have any shootings up there. And I said, Man, I've been here 12 years, and that happened once. It's f*** convenience stores and grocery stores that got massacred. There is a store in New York that got massacred, and did they close down the store in New York?

Dwight: Heck no.

J. White: Or for the schools that get shot up, do they close down the schools after the shooting happens? No. Nobody got killed at my studio; nobody got shot, but because I'm a black business owner, he wants to threaten me and tell me he'll close down my sh*t. So I was like, Damn, I need to get my own property. That's what we're building this for. That's definitely the new goal.

Dwight: Yeah. You've got to get your own, buy the land, and build whatever the hell you want on it. You don't have to pay anybody for the land. You ain't got to pay anyone rent. Everything's covered underneath your business.

J. White: Yeah. That's smart.

Dwight: Yeah. Do you guys have a business coach?

J. White: I use YouTube as my business coach. I learned a lot from YouTube. So, when I'm really in tune, like right now, I'm in my mode, so I'm watching a whole bunch of videos that are in line with my divine purpose, like videos for entrepreneurs. I'm watching Wes Watson talk about how he went to prison for 10 years and then got out four years ago, and he is already a multimillionaire. Guys like that just got super focused, and they focus every day on doing business, so those are like my business coaches and books.

Dwight: Yep. And books. Yep. I don't listen to a lot of music anymore. I listen to a lot of podcasts and learn on YouTube. Google owns YouTube, so it's a great match right there for that. So, everything's on there.

J. White: Yeah, that's where I'm at. That's where I'm at with it too, man. Not a bunch of music, a bunch of education.

Dwight: Yeah, because when I was doing music, writing, and all that stuff, I changed my mindset and my goals to kind of align with the purpose of what I was trying to do and go from there.

J. White: Yes, sir.

Dwight: So, I understand the story behind the Underground Rich Studios, the Rich Girls Museum, the Icy Rich Girls Museum, of course, and the Carolina [26:44 inaudible] clothing line, which are all great businesses. What role do you think failure plays in achieving success?

J. White: It's cold because failure has to happen. It's as necessary as being successful. Every team that's ever played any game definitely loses, but you get up and you learn from losing. So it's a bad thing when you win it. But when you can look back on it and think about the times you lost versus what you gained, it all plays a part. It all makes itself up. You've got to fail in-order to win.

Dwight: Exactly, and that's how we learn, with experience.

J. White: The quicker you fail, the quicker you can win.

Dwight: Facts. The quicker you fail, the quicker you can win. That's a quote right there, too. So, with that, on your road to success, how did you handle the setbacks or obstacles?

J. White: I just handled them as they came, like I told you when we had the music studio and we were having all these artists like Moneybag Yo, Gotti Pull Up, Young Do, and Bankroll Fresh come through my studio in Greensboro, North Carolina. And then I would have my neighbors complain every morning, like, who's going to make Moneybag Yo smoke outside? If Moneybag Yo is in your studio, you're not about to make [28:53] inaudible. So I would say, Fuck it, let him smoke. And then my neighbors would come in the next day and go straight to my landlord with it. So they moved out, and I rented that building, which was an obstacle. Rich Girls Museum grew really fast without any type of promotion. We posted a video on TikTok, and it went viral. And that viral video brought us over a million dollars in revenue, but the next year we tried to open that business in two other markets, and both of them failed. Both markets failed. I mean, we failed before we could even get those things open.

Dwight: What markets?

J. White: It's all types of obstacles. Charlotte, North Carolina, and Myrtle Beach, South Carolina

Dwight: It just wasn't the environment for it.

J. White: Nah, we never got the businesses open. We were just in over our heads. I tried to open three businesses at the same time. I was in three different Rich Girls Museums at the same time, and I didn't have any type of budget strategy. I was just going for it. So they were just really expensive to do. And we didn't have the money to keep going on one of them, the one in Myrtle Beach. But I can play the blame game and blame it on the landlords; like the property in Myrtle Beach, the landlord wasn't there. They assigned me to their architect and told me that I needed to work with their architect to do anything in my business. And their architect wasn't responding, but we were paying five grand a month in rent. And then the one in Charlotte, the one we were building in Charlotte, the rent was six grand a month. So we had 11 grand a month just in rent. And then we started tearing down the one in Charlotte, tearing down the walls that they had, the previous walls, to build the Rich Girls Museum. And we noticed that the roof was leaking really badly, so when I went to the property manager to get the roof fixed, they ended up telling me that they couldn't get the roof fixed and that we signed the as-is agreement. So it was on us to get the roof fixed. So we bowed out of that agreement, and we lost big there. We lost like $65,000 on that building. And we lost 90 grand because I bought a car to put inside the Rich Girls Museum. That was like $25,000 plus the $65,000 we lost remodeling the building. So we lost 90 on that. We lost 40 on the one in Myrtle Beach, and then the Icy Rich Girls Museum, which we built, cost like 200,000. We just kind of ran out of money.

Dwight: You tried to scale too quickly?

J. White: Yeah, exactly.

Dwight: You're going to try for it again at a slow pace, or you're done with it?

J. White: Yeah. Right now, like I told you, me and my girl love to have a good time. We celebrate life every day. We're very happy with each other, so we don't really worry about work too much. We're starting to get into it; we were just thrilled that everything worked out for itself. Rich Girls, we opened that business, and like I said, it made over a million dollars. Then Underground Rich Studios is a million-dollar-a-year business. So just having those businesses, we were fortunate to wake up when we wanted to, go to bed when we wanted to, not really live with discipline, and just have a good time in life. But now we are getting more focused on growing the businesses because we realize we have something really special. I mean, we always knew we had something really special, but we are realizing how much work it takes to really make it successful. And that depends on how we want to grow it. So we're all in the process of trying to grow the business right now.

Dwight: Carolina [34:32 inaudible]. What's your revenue for Carolina [34:36]?

J White: Carolina [34:41 inaudible] is really like a novelty we got in the store, in the underground rich studios, but I mean, it's bringing in 5, 6,000 a month in revenue, not nothing crazy.

Dwight: Okay. You guys weren't trying to get it out. Well, before I even ask you that question, obviously you guys make a great team, and it's hard to find two individuals that work together and sync to make the sh*t that you're doing work and in business too. And it seems that you guys have a plan and a goal. So how do you balance achieving success in your career with other aspects of your life, such as relationships or personal wellbeing?

J. White: Well, it's crazy that you say that right now, like I said, me and her are just really getting focused on just running our businesses together. But if I speak of the past, we had a really fun life. I mean, our staff is young and vibrant. So we're vibrant. I'm a little older. My wife is a little younger. She's 10 years younger than me, so she's still vibrant. So we hang out with the staff; we have businesses that we can hang out at and just have fun at. So working for us is fun. When we're at the studio, we're having a good time. When we're at the Rich Girls Museum, we're having a good time. So the balance is that we are just always having a good time at our jobs, whether we're at home or traveling together. At the Rich Girls Museum, I think we have nine employees. And at Underground Rich, we have about five to seven employees.

Dwight: Okay. And the Carolina [37:09 inaudible] clothing brand just sells itself, and you have customers coming in.

J. White: Yeah. Coming into the studio.

Dwight: Are you guys thinking of branching it out as a separate clothing store or trying to get it into other stores?

J. White: I look at the brand Carolina [37:36 inaudible] like it's going to be around for a hundred plus years. So right now I'm just keeping it consistent with the logo, just keeping it out there. It had a good run in, like, 2019, when I first built it. When I first [38:00 inaudible], a lot of famous artists wanted to wear it, and I got it out there like that. Even recently, Anthony Hamilton wore a hoodie. Tia Kareem wore it on stage. Big Walk Dog wore it. I know somebody was at Glorilla's album release party in New York, and they sent me a video with Glorilla's Manager, who had it on. But as far as how I'm scaling it, I feel like it's a business that's going to be around. I look at Louis Vuitton, and I know the story of Louis Vuitton; I know the story of Gucci; I know the story of like these bigger brands that's been around for a hundred plus years. So I look at it like, This is going to be a brand that's going to be around for a hundred plus years. So I'm not hyped about putting it in other stores. I'm not hyped about overexposing a brand. I just want to be an exclusive brand that grows a reputation through the years.

Dwight: Yep. Word of mouth and marketing just through the Rich Girls Museum and Underground Rich Studios

J. White: I mean, even recently, Lil Tyler had it on. He is a new artist who is blowing up. He had it on his page while he was with Mulatto. He had posted it, and then I reposted it. I like it being an exclusive brand, running it as such, and making it like that. I'm about to pull up to this video shoot. Do you have more questions to ask?

Dwight: I got like one more. I'm going to ask you one more time, and then if I have anything else, I'll text you. So in your opinion, is success a destination or a journey, and why?

J. White: It's definitely a journey because there are all levels of success. If you get a job right now and start a business while you're working, that's a level of success. Like this female named Bree, she cleans businesses. So for years, Bree was working for another company, doing something that she didn't care about, and she hated her job. And then one day she got balls and started calling businesses, saying, Hey, do you need someone to clean your business for you? And I said, Yeah, I do. We worked out a deal, and then at that job [42:20 inaudible], she got paid the same amount or more from me, just one client, and she got to work one week at that job. So she was able to quit that job right away and start working for me. And then, while she was working for me, she picked up other clients. So that's success. But to a multi-billionaire, that ain't success; just starting at the ground level, that's success. So success is a journey because you have to start somewhere and keep going. And the harder you work, the farther you go, and you get to look back at your journey and see all the levels you made it on. I mean, I'm way further along than I was 10 years ago. I'm way further along than I was five years ago.

Dwight: Yep. Definitely. And that's how it is: with every setback, there's a comeback. Your experience Whatever it may be on your path to success, I'm glad you're staying motivated and focused through the challenges. So it's all about balance in achieving success. I thank you for your time, my friend. I appreciate it. I'm going to hit you up later. I'm going to have a landing page on my website. So I'm going to put the link to the Rich Girls Museum on there as well. But in the book, I want to put a couple of pictures of the Rich Girl Museum in the studio as well.

J. White: That's cool. I'm going to send you my number so you have that, and then anything you need, you can just hit me.

Dwight: Okay, cool.

J. White: Alright. I appreciate you.

Dwight: Alright, brother. I appreciate you as well. Thank you.

J. White: How do you think I did in that interview?

Dwight: You did good.

J. White: Okay. I tried to be more resourceful this time. In the last interview I had, my cousin said I wasn't resourceful.

Dwight: You did good. You answered the questions, and a lot of the questions I had, I didn't get to ask you because you already answered them.

J. White: Okay, good, and I was truthful about it too. I was open.

Dwight: Yeah, because you talked about the business. So I have a lot of information here. I recorded our conversation, so I have a lot of information. So I get to go through, sift through, and build that out to put that information in the book.

J. White: Okay. Good deal. So, yeah, just let me know anything else you need; I'm going to text you my number.

Dwight: Thanks, bro. Later.

CHAPTER FOUR
OVERCOMING OBSTACLES AND FAILURE

"Success is not final; failure is not fatal: It is the courage to continue that counts."- Winston Churchill

Obstacles and failures are inevitable on the path to success. They test our resilience, challenge our determination, and provide growth opportunities. Overcoming these hurdles requires a combination of mindset, strategies, and tools. This section will explore ways to navigate obstacles and bounce back from failures, empowering you to continue your journey to success.

COMMON OBSTACLES AND CHALLENGES ON THE ROAD TO SUCCESS

Recognize that obstacles and challenges are part of the journey to success. Some common obstacles an individual encounters include fear of failure, self-doubt, limited resources, lack of support, time constraints, and unexpected setbacks. Each person's journey is unique, and the obstacles may vary.

The first step in overcoming obstacles is acknowledging their existence and reframing them as opportunities for growth. Embrace the mindset that obstacles are temporary roadblocks that can be overcome with the right mindset and strategies.

TOOLS FOR OVERCOMING OBSTACLES

- Mindset Shift: Cultivate a growth mindset that embraces challenges and sees failures as learning opportunities. Challenge negative self-talk and replace it with positive affirmations. Remind yourself that obstacles are steppingstones to success and that Problem-Solving Skills: you have the power to overcome them.

- Develop strong problem-solving skills to tackle obstacles effectively. Break down the obstacle into smaller, more manageable components. Identify potential solutions, brainstorm ideas, and evaluate the pros and cons of each approach. Consider seeking advice or guidance from mentors or experts who have faced similar challenges.

- Resilience Building: Resilience is the ability to bounce back from setbacks and adapt to change. Build resilience by practicing self-care, engaging in activities that recharge you, and surrounding yourself with a supportive network. Cultivate a positive mindset, practice gratitude, and develop coping mechanisms to navigate difficult times.

- Resourcefulness: Take a resourceful approach when faced with limited resources or constraints. Explore alternative solutions, leverage existing resources creatively, and seek collaborations or partnerships. Utilize technology and online platforms to access information, learn new skills, and connect with like-minded individuals who can provide support and guidance.

- Time Management: Effectively managing your time is crucial when facing obstacles. Prioritize your tasks and allocate time for problem-solving and action-taking. Break your goals into smaller, actionable steps and create a realistic timeline. To stay organized and focused, use time management tools, such as calendars, task management apps, or time-tracking techniques.

BOUNCING BACK FROM SETBACKS AND LEARNING FROM FAILURES

Failure is an inevitable part of the success journey. It's essential to approach failures with a growth mindset and view them as valuable learning experiences. Here are tools and strategies to help you bounce back from setbacks and leverage failures for success:

- Reflection and Analysis: Take time to reflect on the failure and analyze what went wrong. Identify the factors that contributed to the setback and the lessons learned. Use this knowledge to adjust your approach, improve, and avoid repeating the same mistakes.

- Adaptability and Flexibility: Embrace adaptability and flexibility when faced with failures. Be open to adjusting your plans, exploring new paths, or revisiting your goals. Adaptability allows for creative problem-solving and encourages innovation in the face of challenges.

- Support System: Surround yourself with a supportive network of individuals who can provide encouragement, guidance, and a fresh perspective. Seek mentors or join communities of like-minded individuals who have experienced similar failures and have overcome them. Engaging with others who can share their stories and insights can help you gain new perspectives and renew your motivation.

- Emotional Resilience: Build emotional resilience to navigate through failures effectively. Acknowledge and accept your emotions, but don't let them consume you. Practice self-compassion and self-care during challenging times. Engage in activities that help you rejuvenate and regain your emotional balance, such as exercise, meditation, or spending time in nature.

- Continuous Learning and Growth: Embrace a continuous learning and growth mindset. View failures as opportunities to learn, improve, and refine your strategies. Seek feedback from others, analyze successful case studies, and invest in personal and professional development. The more knowledge and skills you acquire, the better equipped you will be to overcome obstacles and achieve success.

Remember, overcoming obstacles and failure is not a linear process. It requires persistence, adaptability, and a willingness to learn from setbacks. Utilize the tools and strategies mentioned above to navigate obstacles, bounce back from failures, and keep on your path to success. Embrace challenges as opportunities for growth and maintain a positive mindset that fuels your resilience and determination. With perseverance and the right tools, you can overcome any obstacle and achieve your desired success.

TOOLS FOR OVERCOMING OBSTACLES AND FAILURE

- Visualization: Visualization is a powerful tool that creates vivid mental images of successfully overcoming obstacles and achieving your goals. Take time each day to visualize yourself facing challenges confidently, finding solutions, and celebrating your success. This practice helps to rewire your brain, boost your confidence, and reinforce a positive mindset.

- Supportive Networks: Surround yourself with a supportive network of individuals who believe in your abilities and can provide guidance and encouragement during difficult times. Seek mentors and coaches or join mastermind groups where you can learn from others' experiences, share insights, and receive support.

- Emotional Intelligence: Develop emotional intelligence to effectively manage your emotions in the face of obstacles and failures. Emotional intelligence involves understanding and regulating your emotions and empathizing with others. Cultivate self-awareness, practice emotional regulation techniques, and enhance your interpersonal skills. This will help you navigate challenging situations with grace and maintain positive relationships.

- Adaptability and Flexibility: Cultivate adaptability and flexibility to navigate unexpected obstacles and plan changes. Learn to embrace uncertainty and view challenges as opportunities for growth and innovation. Develop a mindset that welcomes change and seeks alternative solutions when faced with roadblocks.

- Resilience Practices: Incorporate resilience-building practices into your daily routine. This may include journaling, practicing gratitude, engaging in physical exercise, seeking inspiration from motivational books or podcasts, or engaging in activities that bring you joy and relaxation. These practices help you build inner strength, maintain a positive outlook, and bounce back from setbacks.

Overcoming obstacles and failure requires perseverance, resilience, and a growth mindset. It's essential to consistently utilize these tools and strategies, adapt them to your unique circumstances, and seek continuous personal and professional growth. By doing so, you will be better equipped to overcome challenges, learn from failures, and ultimately achieve your desired success.

PRACTICAL EXERCISE

CULTIVATING RESILIENCE

Instructions: Identify a recent setback or failure you experienced. Reflect on the lessons learned from that experience and write them down. Consider applying those lessons to bounce back stronger and overcome future challenges. Use the Resilience Reflection Worksheet (Example Worksheet 2) to guide your reflection.

CHAPTER FIVE
BUILDING A SUPPORT SYSTEM

"Your ability to communicate is an important tool in your pursuit of your goals, whether it is with family, your coworkers, or your clients and customers."
-Steve Harvey

The journey toward success can be difficult, but it is not a solo journey and it's important to have a support system to help you achieve your goals. A support system can consist of a network of people who can offer guidance, advice, and encouragement along the way. This chapter will discuss the importance of having a support system to help you succeed.

NETWORKING

Networking is an essential component of building a support system. It involves meeting people and building relationships with them, which can help you in your personal and professional life. Networking can be done in various ways, such as attending industry events, joining professional organizations, and connecting with people on social media. By networking, you can meet people who can offer advice, mentorship, and even job opportunities.

One benefit of networking is that it allows you to learn from others who have gone before you. You can learn from their experiences, mistakes, and successes, which can help you to avoid common pitfalls and make better decisions. Networking can also help you build your reputation and establish yourself as a trusted and knowledgeable professional.

MENTORSHIP

Mentorship is another important aspect of building a support system. A mentor can offer guidance, advice, and support as you work toward your goals. They can help you to develop your skills, provide feedback on your work, and offer insights into the industry or field you are working in.

Finding a mentor can be challenging, but it's worth the effort. You can start by looking for people who have succeeded in your field or industry. You can also ask for recommendations from colleagues or friends. When approaching a potential mentor, it's important to respect their time and expertise. Also be clear about what you hope to gain from the mentorship relationship.

LIKE-MINDED INDIVIDUALS

Finding like-minded individuals is another important aspect of building a support system. These are people who share your interests, goals, and values. They can offer support, encouragement, and inspiration as you work toward your goals.

You can find like-minded individuals in various ways, such as joining online communities, attending events and conferences, or participating in group activities. When looking for like-minded individuals, being open-minded and willing to engage with people from diverse backgrounds and experiences is important.

BENEFITS OF A SUPPORT SYSTEM

- A support system can offer numerous benefits as you work toward your goals. For example, it can give you a sense of belonging and community. It can also help you stay motivated and accountable, as you have people invested in your success. A support system can also offer different perspectives and insights, which can help you to make better decisions and solve problems more effectively.

- A support system can provide individuals with the guidance, resources, and motivation needed to achieve their goals. Building a strong support system requires effort and time, but the benefits are worth it. The following are additional components to building a strong support system.

- Identify your needs: Before building a support system, it is important to identify one's needs. This can include identifying areas where one needs guidance, resources, or motivation. By identifying one's needs, individuals can focus on building a support system that meets their specific needs.

- Diversify your support system: A strong support system should consist of diverse individuals. This can include individuals with different backgrounds, experiences, and perspectives. By diversifying one's support system, individuals can gain new insights and perspectives, which can help them achieve their goals.

- Be a supportive member: Building a support system is a two-way street. Individuals should also be willing to provide support to others. By supporting others, individuals can build relationships and establish connections that can lead to new opportunities.

- Communicate effectively: Effective communication is key to building a strong support system. By effectively communicating one's needs, goals, and challenges, individuals can ensure that their support system provides the help and resources they need.

Remember, success is not a solo journey; building a strong support system can make all the difference.

PRACTICAL EXERCISE

MAPPING YOUR SUPPORT NETWORK
INSTRUCTIONS:

- Use a paper or open a blank document on your computer.

- Start by listing the areas of your life where you could benefit from having a support system, such as career, personal development, health, relationships, and hobbies.

- For each area, brainstorm the different types of support you might need. This could include emotional support, knowledge or expertise, accountability, encouragement, or networking opportunities.

- Once you have identified the types of support you need, think about the people in your life who could provide that support. These can be family members, friends, colleagues, mentors, or even online communities or groups related to your interests.

- Create a visual representation of your support network by drawing a diagram or using a mind-mapping tool. Write the names of the people who form part of your support system in the specific areas where they can offer support.

- Reflect on your support network and identify gaps or areas where you may need to expand your connections.

- Consider how to nurture and strengthen your existing relationships within your support network. Think about ways you can give back and support others as well.

- Set an action plan for contacting individuals within your support system. Determine how you will engage with them and communicate your needs and goals.

- Regularly review and update your support network as your needs and circumstances change. Stay open to expanding your network and seeking new connections that align with your evolving goals and aspirations.

CHAPTER 6:
CAREER SUCCESS

"Choose a job you love, and you will never have to work a day in your life."
– Confucius

Career success is a highly desirable outcome for many individuals. It brings a sense of accomplishment, financial stability, and personal satisfaction. The importance of career success cannot be overstated, as it can positively affect one's overall quality of life. Achieving career success requires dedication, hard work, and a clear understanding of what success means to you. This article will discuss the importance of career success and how to achieve it.

FINDING A FULFILLING CAREER

The first step to achieving career success is finding a career that aligns with your interests, values, and skills. A fulfilling career can bring a sense of purpose and satisfaction, making staying motivated and engaged in your work easier. You can start by exploring your interests and passions to find a fulfilling career. What do you enjoy doing? What are you good at? What kind of impact do you want to make in the world? These questions can help guide you toward a career that aligns with your values and goals.

BUILDING SKILLS AND EXPERTISE

Once you have identified a career path that interests you, building the skills and expertise is essential. This may involve pursuing additional education or training, gaining practical experience, or developing a strong network of professionals in your field. Building your skills and expertise can make you a more competitive candidate for job opportunities, and it can also increase your confidence and sense of competence in your work.

ADVANCING IN YOUR CAREER

Advancing in your career is another critical component of achieving career success. This may involve taking on new responsibilities, pursuing leadership roles, or seeking promotions within your organization. To advance in your career, you must demonstrate a strong work ethic, a willingness to learn and grow, and the ability to work well with others. Developing a strategic plan for your career and setting clear goals for yourself is also essential. This can help you stay focused and motivated as you work toward achieving your career aspirations.

NETWORKING AND BUILDING RELATIONSHIPS

Networking and building relationships are important aspects of achieving career success. Building a strong professional network can provide access to job opportunities, mentorship, and valuable insights into your field. To build your network, you can attend industry events, join professional organizations, and connect with colleagues and peers on social media platforms like LinkedIn.

MAINTAINING A WORK-LIFE BALANCE

Achieving career success does not come at the expense of your personal life. Maintaining a healthy work-life balance is critical for well-being and career success. This may involve setting boundaries between work and personal time, prioritizing self-care, and engaging in hobbies and activities outside of work.

Achieving career success requires hard work, dedication, and strategic planning. Finding a fulfilling career, building skills and expertise, advancing your career, networking and building relationships, and maintaining a healthy work-life balance are all important components of career success. By focusing on these areas, you can build a rewarding and fulfilling career that aligns with your values and goals.

PRACTICAL EXERCISE

PERSONAL MISSION STATEMENT

INSTRUCTIONS

- Reflect on your career aspirations, values, and passions.

- Write a personal mission statement that encapsulates your purpose and goals in your career.

- Consider what impact you want to make, the values you want to uphold, and the skills you want to develop.

- Craft a concise and meaningful statement that represents your career direction and serves as a guiding principle.

- Review and refine your mission statement, ensuring it aligns with your values and resonates with your aspirations.

Now Let's Hear From A Driven Entrepreneur With Multiple Businesses, Seeking Guidance From Social Media Influencers. He Mentors A Young Couple And Believes Success Is A Continuous Journey. He Plans To Expand His Businesses And Replicate The Model In Various Locations. Gabriel Acknowledges The Sacrifices He Must Make To Achieve His Goals.

https://eclipseloungeandbar.com/
https://alohabreezerentals.com/

Focused, determined,
and ready to conquer the
business world

- Courtesy of Gabriel Francois

Dwight: All right. Yeah. So, I just got to record the audio because I had to transcribe it. So, I'll have a record of it that makes it easy for me to do the narrative for the book. So, I'm just going to ask you questions. So first, I'm writing a book called Success Has Receipts, and basically, it's showing the reader that success is attainable. It's out there for them to attain as long as they stay focused, ready, and available. Whether it's gathering whatever resources or the connections that they need to make in whatever field that they choose to venture in, whatever it may be, they know that on the road to success, there are ups and downs, but some of the rewards of success are perseverance and setbacks. It's the things that it takes to get there that make it successful, and they're not always guaranteed. There are always ups and downs in success. So, it'll give them some smart goals, some things that they can achieve by writing down their objectives and stuff and getting to the goals. So, I just want to give them the perspective of someone who did it. Destination From folks that made because, because for me, success is a journey; it's not a destination Continue to build and continue to take it one step at a time in order to reach your goals, personal or professional. So, tell me, who is Gabriel Francois?

Gabriel: Alright, Gabriel Francois. Where should I start? I think Gabriel Francios, just someone who pretty much grew up in an inner city but always knew at an early age he didn't want to work as tiring as his parents did for the rest of his life. So, he just has to basically figure out how I was going to go ahead and get financial freedom. Currently it's a near ending chase because sometimes you set a goal to get somewhere, and then when you reach that goal, you want to attain something bigger. So, Gabriel Francis, just someone who wants financial freedom and he'll basically go to any means attain that goal. Reason why? My main purpose to actually go ahead and seek betterment and also financial freedom for my son. I always want the next generation to actually do better, so that's like my main purpose right now to set a foundation so when he grows up, he could have choices I didn't have growing up.

Dwight: When did the idea of financial freedom come to you?

Gabriel: So, financial freedom I think it all clicked. I think it was the summer after I graduated from high school. I already had a summer job and everything, and pretty much it was just moving on to school. But growing up, I always had, like, my Uncle John, who would come over and you have like a side hustle or a business that pretty much he'll try to sell or promote. So, growing up, I was always surrounded by stuff like that. But the one that actually clicked was when I had to help my brother Lyle for Labor Day, and I saw how, at that point, he was selling a nutritional drink called Zenga at the time. I remember that. We stay out all day, pretty much in Brooklyn, during Labor Day. And he would sell almost anything.

He ran out of Zango and they were selling just regular stuff that they had brought up, supplies that they had brought out there, and people were still buying just that. And then also, I think I started out following in the footsteps of, like, an Amazon store, and it just took off from there. Once I saw how to set it up and how easy it was, it wasn't easy at first, but it was still attainable, and I didn't have to really answer to anyone. I started pursuing entrepreneurship even more after that. From then on, it's just been developing, learning from mistakes, and continuing because, as I said before, in entrepreneurship or financial freedom, every time you set a goal, you reach that goal, you come close to attaining that goal, and you set another goal that's higher. So, I believe it's never-ending. At some point, you'll basically get to slow down a little bit, but as of right now, I'm still chasing it.

Dwight: So, let's get into your first successful business, and that's the one that you have in Hawaii, which is The Touro business, right? Was that your first successful business?

Gabriel: I would say no; I'd say the one that started off was my Amazon store. I started the Amazon store when I was, as I said, right out of high school. It started out with just selling memory cards, but the return on investment was great. I didn't really have to focus on, you know, my summer job or pretty much my job while I started school because I was just selling memory cards. At an early age, I found out how to go ahead and buy all the supplies from Shenzen, China, and then ship them over. I would sell the items in bulk or pretty much loose. But, I think for me, that was the first one, the first success. The return on investments was pretty high, and yet it wasn't a crowded market at all, so I was able to capitalize pretty well for the area.

Dwight: Do you still have that Amazon store?

Gabriel: No, I've stopped that. I think I stopped selling stuff on Amazon the year after I joined the Army because at that point stuff was going well, but I needed a lot of internal support, and I didn't have that, so as far as keeping up with the store, it didn't work out. So, I basically just evolved and moved on. But every base that I went to since then, I would look at the area and see something that I didn't have, and I would transform myself to actually go ahead and provide that need, and it's been working ever since.

Dwight: So that was when Touro was worth it for you?

Gabriel: So pretty much with Touro, I liked to travel too, so pretty much I took a trip to LA, and I took Airbnb and all that stuff, and Hertz didn't have the car that I wanted. I didn't really like the car anyway, or the options that they had. So, I checked it out. I was just doing a random search, and I stumbled upon Touro. And if you guys don't know about Touro, it's like Airbnb for cars. So, when they first came out, they had, I think when I went to LA, prices for a luxurious car, but you could get the same thing for like a subcompact. So I went with the luxurious car, and I had a lot of fun, and I thought it was a good idea. So once I went back, I was in Alaska at that time, so once I got back off leave, I posted my Jeep because Alaska, if you guys don't know, especially Fairbanks, has one of the biggest ice sculpting competitions annually, and they would pretty much rent all the cars out, and they'd have to basically have trucks transport rental cars in the wintertime, which took a long time. And then yet still, it was supply and demand, so you'll see a regular compact rental go from, let's say, $40 a day to, like, $250 for one day, so I definitely took advantage of that.

I started out with one car, but then I didn't really use that car that much. I had another friend that lived in the same apartment complex, and we'd just carpool out to work. So, I just kept on; I started renting that car out, and then it wasn't until I got to Hawaii that I really started basically expanding out. I think the first month of operations in Hawaii, I had a 2011 Jeep Grand Cherokee, and I think it was like a thousand dollars. And to me, it was just like, okay, I rode my motorcycle. So, it didn't really affect me much. But then I saw the need for the rental, so I said to myself, I'll go ahead and reinvest for the next six months. I'll take the profits and reinvest them back into what I do as far as supplies. And then I found, like, pretty much car auctions. I leveraged myself in a way so my LLC could basically act as a dealership, and I was able to go ahead and purchase cars from the auctions every month.

It started every month. I purchased probably one car, cleaned it up, and then put it back on the road. I put a future on it, and before you know it, I think I went from just that one car to about six to eight cars right before the pandemic. And then leading up to it, I think the highest I had at that time for that year was probably 17 to 18 cars. And yeah, it got addicted after that; pretty much I just kept on reinvesting, but still, at that time, I could start leveraging, save more, and then develop a business plan, which I did. During the pandemic, you would think that once they shut down everything, no one would go anywhere. But for a lot of locals, they basically started renting the cars when they stopped having vacations. It was a little route, but still, I found a way to actually make it out of it.

I transformed the business itself, so I catered more to nurses who were traveling then. And then there were also just locals that didn't have a car at the time, so I still have me afloat, but it wasn't until they start-ed lifting travel bans for flights and travelers coming into Hawaii that everything took off because again, it was supply and demand. Hertz and all the other big-name companies had [unclear 20:35] through the pandemic to try to leverage their businesses. And locals definitely had a good situation; they were put in a good situation. I had a good credit score, so I went ahead. The biggest mistake that I regret in entrepre-neurship is basically purchasing the cards under my personal credit. It affected it for a little while, but knowing what I know now about business credit, I wish I had pretty much doubled upon that before I started buying cars.

It was pretty addictive. So I found out that, pretty much if you go to one dealership, you find out which credit bureau and which bank they actually go ahead and look at. You can purchase, you basically just get a loan, and you purchase one or two cars from that dealership, routed to different banks. I went down the street, and I was like, Oh, two cars, that's fine. Started putting them on the road that same day and booking like crazy. I had bookings for, like, up to six months just in the first week of listing them.

Dwight: So, in your first year of business, what was your revenue?

Gabriel: Like I said, but the first year of business, I think for Touro itself, the first year in Hawaii, or the first year?

Dwight: Hawaii. Yeah. Hawaii is when it really took off, right?

Gabriel: Yeah. So, the first year, I think it may have been because I only had, at the end of that year, probably 8 to 10 cars, but mainly I started out with just that one car. I think anywhere from probably 30 to probably 35,000, which is not bad, but when you factor in the cost for cleaning, in between gas and maintenance, it [unclear 23:09], but after that, I went from that amount, and then basically, after the pandemic, it went from about a year to like every two months or that pretty much one month, it made close to that. When I say I made that amount, again, it doesn't factor in cost. I think I had the most cars at that time, so it was pretty much, you had to factor in gas, you had to factor in maintenance, you had to factor, they were stealing cars back then in Hawaii, like really bad. So, they stole one of my cars, and they definitely trashed it, and it was left on me, not the insurance companies. So, I had to go ahead and rectify that, but it was still a good situation to be in.

Dwight: So, you scaled pretty quick, which allowed you to capitalize on the market there?

Gabriel: Yeah.

Dwight: And did you have to scale back at some point?

Gabriel: I did have to scale back. I think for me, once I saw Hawaii taking off, I went in and put in an extension because I was stationed there. So, I put in an extension to actually stay in Hawaii for, I think, one to two extra years. At the time of the pandemic, it was slowing down the PCS process, so I thought I was safe. So, my main plan was to basically extend for two more years. And then in those two years, basically, leverage like business credit and all that stuff but coming down towards, I think it was about six months afterwards, it didn't go through. I had orders to cut out before, and I was going like all over on the other side of America to [unclear 25:38], and I exactly had to go ahead and sell most of my cars, sell, trade, because at that time I was just working by myself with one or two other helpers, like working out.

But I knew at that point that they wouldn't be able to handle the load or pretty much have the same effect that I had by myself. So, I went ahead and sold some of the cars so it wouldn't be a burden to them. And I wouldn't run into a failure issue, but although I did that, it didn't turn into a failure, but it slowed down drastically after I left because, one thing I tell somebody, pretty much the vision that you have for your business, no one else would have that. No one will have that passion. No one will have that enthusiasm to basically improve and develop things like customer service or the quality of your property. So afterwards I had to definitely dissect and cut down from close to like 24 cars just to go down to like 10 or 12, and now I'm at just six right now.

Dwight: And that comment you just made about someone else having the same drive or the same mindset as you when it comes to your business is because it's your baby, right?

Gabriel: Exactly.

Dwight: You started it; you created it. You put your blood, sweat, and tears into it, but you can instill that in them. You can teach them and show them how to operate the business and achieve success, and you can be a mentor to that person as well. So, when they are done working with you, they can have that driving passion and put it into something that they want to do. I think as entrepreneurs, we have to be able to teach others and show them how to be entrepreneurs as well. So, they have the same driving passion as we do. We've got to mentor them that way, because one day they're not going to stay working for you forever. So, you want them to have the same drive and motivation as you do in your business. But again, nobody's going to outwork me in my own business, per se. You just have to instill that in them so that they have the same drive and passion. You teach them, coach them, and mentor them, just like we do in the military.

Gabriel: Exactly. Yeah.

Dwight: So that way, one day they can be successful because for me, I want everybody; my mindset is that everybody should be an entrepreneur because the way the government is, or America is, they teach you to work. You get stuck being an employee more than a business owner.

Gabriel: Exactly.

Gabriel: The combination you just said as far as, like, everyone should have some kind of entrepreneurial skills is good, but still, as you also said, most people are just brainwashed into just doing a nine-to-five, being acceptable, going home, and just living that story until they have to retire or die. But just the drive of financial freedom, being able to travel without even thinking twice, or basically taking different opportunities to spend more time with family or your loved ones That's like the biggest thing ever in entrepreneurship. But not everyone is going to have that at all. You have people that I know that I've seen, like in the military, who, if they took entrepreneurship seriously or if that was their path, would be like 10 times better than me. But yet still, there are a lot of people who are just comfortable with the regular and staying within [unclear30:57].

Dwight: Yeah. So, touch on this: what year did you join the military?

Gabriel: I joined in January 2009.

Dwight: And then you, at your first duty station, which was Fort Stewart, Georgia, had no idea about entrepreneurship until you went to Alaska, correct?

Gabriel: No, remember, I started at the Amazon store.

Dwight: What year did you start Amazon?

Gabriel: That was before the military? Like 2007 and 2008, within Alaska. Alaska was, after I stopped with the Amazon store and liquidations and all that stuff on eBay, where I started fixing cell phones and tablets, and that transferred to Alaska. because, like once I went to Alaska, it had one, probably one cell phone repair. And the other one was all the way, like six hours away in Anchorage. So definitely, again, supply and demand, offering maybe something that's not commonly found there. I did that for a little while, and it turned out to be good because in the wintertime I'll have, like, right after I get off work, I'll basically pick my son up from the Boys and Girls Club. We'll probably get like dinner or something like that, and right after, all the way from, I'd say, probably around seven all the way to about like 12, he'll have people lined up just waiting to get their cell phone or account fixed or unlocked, and then I started buying and selling phones. So that definitely turned out to be something good for that area at that time.

Dwight: What year was that?

Gabriel: That was from 2014 to 2018.

Dwight: Okay. And then Touro started in 2018?

Gabriel: Yeah, 2017, 2018.

Dwight: So, you touched on some specific failures and setbacks and your experiences on your path to success and bouncing back from each of those ventures that you started. And how has failure contributed to your personal growth and ultimately helped you achieve greater success?

Gabriel: I think failure is one of the things that, as an entrepreneur, you look at, and sometimes people run away. They don't like failing, but still, failure is just; it gives you everything that you need to go ahead and develop yourself as a human being and as an entrepreneur. I think the biggest failure I had was, basically, working by myself. I think we touched on it a little bit. Now I realize that, pretty much, you have to basically recreate yourself to maximize your effort and maximize your true potential. That was one of the biggest failure flaws because I'm naturally to myself; like, pretty much, I don't like the whole crowd, the lights, and all that stuff every single time. So, when it came time for pretty much any of the business that I did before, I think it was one time I grabbed my son up and had him help out.

He was always there for my assistance, but I needed to branch out a lot more. And with that being said, like today's entrepreneurial endeavor out here at Fort Drum, pretty much I started with just three people, and I reemphasize everything—all the goals and everything that they were supposed to go ahead and do. And basically, give them a task and a little bit of free room so they can add their personal touch to it. And that was like one of the best decisions that I made. Other than that, the failure probably reshaped my whole entrepreneurial skill-set. The failure of just like failure in life for me, I don't consider it a true failure in life if you're still working for someone else this long and you're only cut out to have like 12 to 14 days of vacation when they tell you you can have that.

And for me, being dependent on that for so many years, it seemed like a failure. So now I'm definitely taking all the actions to go ahead and make sure I don't have to do it much longer. I'll have my own free room and my own time. Your time is like one of the main things—the main essence—in entrepreneurship and in life. Like, whoever controls your time controls your whole livelihood and your whole demeanor. So, I figure if I take that power off my time, that pretty much puts me in a position where I ultimately want to be.

Dwight: Okay. definitely. You have that entrepreneurial spirit in you, and you instilled it in other people, like your son, as you mentioned, and as well as your employees, right? Giving them the kind of autonomy to go ahead and be an added value to your business makes them feel like they're contributing to something, and it's not all your ideas. You make them feel invested in your business and make them want to work for you as well. So, let's segue into that. So, tell me how many employees you have currently, as far as I know, with the new business and the club, and then segue into the second business you're opening, but touch on how many employees you have. When did that part of your entrepreneurial journey start? Because you said, as you look at the market, wherever you are stationed, which you're now stationed at Fort Drum, New York, you see what's not there and what you can add to, whether it's the community or the area that you're in, and you kind of capitalize on that market and then scale on a larger level. So, talk about that.

Gabriel: So pretty much the current market I'm in right now, I don't think I ever wanted growing up, I never wanted to be like a club owner or a lounge owner. It kind of just basically stumbled upon my life; I think car rental was still doing well. I was helping with that during my deployment. I wake up like three in the morning, and basically, I go out and take care of customer service calls, but on one of those calls I had a soldier that, pretty much, I didn't even know they were listening to the call; they were like in a bunker, and they were like, man, that's pretty neat, like what you're doing. I hear it from time to time, like, you ever thought about doing stuff like that in Watertown, New York? I was like, Yeah, there are no rentals over there. I really don't see any. I was just trying to go ahead and just do my time and just move on from Watertown.

But later on, that week, when the soldiers came back to me, they were like, they have a lounge that would be perfect. They're going out of business because they didn't run it properly. But it's the only thing that soldiers, locals, and the younger crowd have to go to because, still, they only have one regular bar that is in that vicinity. And yeah, they definitely didn't like it at all. So, what we did was just sit down, it was one of my direct soldiers, she went in, she got all the info, she brought it back, and we started with just two people. And those same two people, with whom I'm still in business today, gave me a lot of time. They gave me a lot of ideas because, as I said before, club life was never really my thing. As an entrepreneur, you should always evolve to achieve success.

So, I think that's one of the main things that I like about entrepreneurship. It gives you motivation and the drive to evolve and do something somewhat better. So, we started plans. I told him we were going to run it like a training meeting. So, army training meetings, we do them all the way up to six months, sometimes a year. So, what we did was start the plan, and I will never forget this; it was my [unclear 42:33]. So, they came in, we sat down in a small enclosed place; it's just like a container that they turned into a room, and we went through different marketing strategies to see how we'll go ahead and open up, which will be the first day when the pre-launch will be what we are going to do in the next six to eight months.

Dwight: Backup plan.

Gabriel: Exactly. We're doing a lot of backup planning. It wasn't even like higher up or high ranking; it was just lower enlisted that knew the crowd, they knew the experience, and when they were in there from time to time, they knew the true potential of it, and it was definitely a blessing to go ahead and be able to just start off with two people. Once we got back on the ground, it was kind of hard to navigate everything, which could be miles away. But I really enjoy that because it helps you think outside the box to be more effective as just a leader or just an entrepreneur itself, working on a business from miles away where you don't have the full effect, you don't have the time because mostly everybody takes you more seriously when you're physically there. So if you're able to still move and make moves from miles away, it definitely answers your needs as an entrepreneur because you're not supposed to be in that dwelling every single day.

There comes a point where you have to go ahead and learn how to go ahead and make moves or think ahead. So my main thing is just, basically, thinking ahead of time. That's what helped me a lot, and that's what helped shape this chapter of my entrepreneurship.

Dwight: Because you're dealing with the time difference, You're dealing with two different personalities. Three, you have to, again, like you said, think outside the box and have somebody have the ability. You have to know your people and have somebody be there representing you. Now, did they invest in the business with you, or was it just

Gabriel: No, they invested their time. What I did felt, as I said, like I had to go ahead and downsize. So I took most of the cars that I bought, sold them, and put them into the new business, basically using them as a write-off. The only thing that I requested from them was their time and then scheduling. They help schedule a lot of stuff in between as far as having the right people, because if you have a club and you don't have the right people in there, you're going to have pretty much just a dry club. So we went in and scheduled a lot of influences in the area to come through and set up a time for them to come through so people could see them in there, and that's the way. I track a vast number of soldiers and civilians.

Dwight: So while you were building that business, you were paying them for their time, correct?

Gabriel: When we were first starting off, I didn't pay them at all. Before we opened up, leading up, it was just, we all knew it was going to turn out good, so we didn't focus too much on that. That's one thing we sat down on, and I said, I can't give you guys a lot of money or anything like that for your time right now, before we opened. So they volunteered a lot of their time, so painting, setting the building because the building was like, it was horrible when I first came back. I came back, and it needed a lot of construction done to the building. The last owner cut a lot of pipes out. They messed up the electric as far as the structure inside the building—a lot of stuff that made the space, like, very small. What I had to do at that point, again, evolved. So we came back, and I never really did that much construction work. I never did electrical work.

But all in all, I learned how to do it because we didn't have that many contractors out here. So I had to go ahead and figure out how to do stuff and align myself with a couple of people who couldn't take that workload on. And they came in; we had charge until we opened. Then, when we opened, I turned them from just associates to managers. So they manage almost all the events. And I just came up with a plan that I issued out, and they kept it afloat.

Dwight: Okay. Yeah. Because when you're not there, you have to trust that the employees are going to run it the way that you want it. But then giving them some autonomy, again, like I said, so that they feel invested and want to be there because they trust you and the process, So what habits or routines have you found helpful in achieving your goals?

Gabriel: I would say writing it down So pretty much, with entrepreneurship, the main thing that keeps you motivated is looking at the end state. So for instance, on my phone, I usually have a picture of something, like a collage. It was like, One is family. And then my first true love was a realtor. I definitely wanted to go into real estate and basically buy and flip houses, but it's a step-by-step process to have the revenue to go ahead. For me, at that point, the mindset was, Okay, well, I'm starting this business off. And then after that, that's when I'll jump on back to real estate and go ahead and do that. So, on my phone, I did, like, an early collage, probably four or five years ago. One was pretty much how many homes I needed to have to be financially free. So at that point, I wanted 20, 26, and So pretty much, I had one picture with that, and I had the number 26 on it.

So if a random person looks at my phone and they look at the wallpaper, they're like, What the hell is this? But to me, it made sense. It gave me that motivation: family 26. But now, as times change pretty much, I have Trucking—I definitely want to get into that. Everything is activated, but still, as far as the lounge or club, that one is strong, car rentals are on there, family is on there, and I just look at that every single time. Even when you look to see what time of day it is, it's a constant reminder. Okay, well, this is what I have to do, but leading into that, I started writing out all my plans. It's like a web, pretty much. So now I have a six-foot dry erase board. And I started out my new web by pretty much taking the restaurants; the lounge now involves like a restaurant or club at night, and then it has the lounge right next to it as a separate entity. So I just started to work on that. And it's just daily reminders. When you walk past it and take a picture, you look through it, and it keeps you accountable for those goals.

Dwight: Okay. Definitely. Seeing it written down, and you're right, when I write down what I'm going to do, the process, especially when it came to writing this book, just writing down each thing that I'm going to do every day to get to finishing and completing the book, whatever it may be, you want to see it written down and you can check it off and say, hey, like at work. I write down everything on the board that I have to accomplish, and once it's accomplished, I put a tick mark on it, or I erase it off the board and add something else. So yeah, you have to have some type of accountability. Because if you don't have somebody keeping you accountable or if you're not keeping yourself accountable, you're bound to not focus much on those aspects or those things that you need to accomplish. So now you've talked about the club and how you're scaling that into a restaurant or lounge, and just recently you started another venture. What is that? You've started to scale?

Gabriel: Can you say it again?

Dwight: You started to scale into another business?

Gabriel: So yeah, pretty much that's where the restaurant comes into play.

Dwight: And that's what you're working on now?

Gabriel: Exactly. Yeah. So I saw again that the area doesn't; it's predominantly a white neighborhood. And it's an older neighborhood too. So pretty much most people that come here just do their time, they leave out, but they don't have a Caribbean restaurant. They don't have soul food. They don't have a lot of trendy new menus that you would typically have in an inner-city area or just basically somewhere else. They do have okay restaurant trains, but as far as diversity, they don't; it's just one set menu all the way through. You go to all the restaurants, and they have pretty much the same thing. So I saw that the nightlife is great, but if you capitalize, I saw one place in Queens, New York, that's where I travel and also plays a big role in it.

Once you go to different places, you see different ways of life and get so many ideas. So that's the other thing that I'm grateful and thankful for, but it's this one spot in Queens, New York. It's a restaurant by day, but the way they have it set up, it's a classy, good restaurant you can take your family to during the daytime, but once 10 o'clock hits, the lights cut down and it turns into a mini nightclub. They still sell food, but they also sell a better vibe, and that's what I'm trying to capitalize on right now.

Dwight: Does the menu change at night, or is it the same throughout?

Gabriel: Yeah, the menu changes at night. That's like VIP, and if you want a certain menu, that's when you could change over. So there's not a big demand for making a full menu list at night. It's just a smaller crowd that pays more because they want diversity. And I'm trying it out right now in the new location, and it's doing well. One marketing strategy I did was, sometimes you have trial and error; you try a lot of different things, but this one was, what should I say? We basically cut down the stock, so like the oxtails and all the stuff that everybody wanted or gravitated to, we cut it down, so instead of doing a full stock, we did a small portion. So once they come in, they smell the food. Oh yeah, we want this. What do you have, oxtail? They look up on the menu, they want this, they want that, and it'll be gone in like an hour or an hour and a half.

Dwight: Sorry, not to cut you off, but once it's gone, that's it.

Gabriel: Yeah. So what it did was force people to come out earlier, and they started telling all their friends, Oh yeah, they have good oxtail; they have good Caribbean food over there. So it had people that were just coming to buy plates, like white people that are just coming to buy plates. Take that out of the book. Don't say that. They were coming in to buy food and all that stuff, and if the crowd or the vibe for the night wasn't their thing, they still walked through the door and bought food. That's one of the main things that we started doing. But now I believe that we're ready. I'm moving on to, like, Door Dash and Uber Eats over the summer, and then the restaurant should be up and running pretty soon.

Dwight: So yeah. Oh, so you didn't get another establishment? It's the same establishment?

Gabriel: No, right now it's the same establishment, but we did move to a bigger location. So, one thing just to get our foot in the door, like I just focused on the same spot that everybody knows as far as creating that lounge or whatever. And then I had time to look at different structures, and I recently found one where I'm able to do the hookah lounge on one side because what they have at the bar is that it's just for 21 and above. So the 21 and below had nowhere to go, so I created the hookah lounge just specifically for everybody, but the older crowd doesn't like congregating with the 18-year-olds and all that. So I figure if we had both in one spot, one for 21 and above and the other for 18 and below, One serves liquor, one doesn't. Exactly. I capitalized on both.

Dwight: So you changed locations, essentially.

Gabriel: So I'm currently moving. So the moving process, especially for a new business, is kind of hard because, again, all of this is self-funded. You're just leveraging some opportunities that are bestowed on you, but right now I couldn't move my liquor license as fast because I just applied for it, so I'm still waiting on that process to go through. But I started construction work, so by the time all the paperwork falls through, The hookah will be the first one because you don't really need that much paperwork to dive into that. So that's the first one, and it should launch probably in the next three weeks. But that's like your after-hours spot. They could close down at two if the crowd liked it or wanted to do something afterwards. So I'm definitely opening up the doors for them starting in the next few weeks. So once we close down the bar area, they'll go to the new location. They'll go to the hookah lounge at 4:00 a.m.

Dwight: Do you currently have a mentor or business coach?

Gabriel: Currently, I don't. It's weird. I feel like, for me, I wouldn't say I don't. I have people I look up to on social media, and I look at the different strategies that they talk about. Because there are a lot of people that give, social media is good and it's also bad, but one of the main things I like about social media is that it has a lot of people, especially those just starting out, and when you're just starting out, they give you a lot of free games before they start charging you for a little advice. So that's what I find, like different groups that are doing the same movements as me, but they are just doing it on a bigger level. I also reached out just for this venue. As far as that, this one restaurant in Queens that I reached out to actually followed my page first, and I was like, Bro, they have over 10,000 true followers. They followed my page, and after that, I was like, I started looking at stuff that they had, and we went back and forth.

So, we're supposed to actually have a meeting in the next month or so. I'm going down there to see exactly what's going on, how they run and set up stuff, and check out other spots that are in their area as well. In the sense of mentorship, I look at different businesses or the dream I have for mine, and I just basically focus in and lock in on that. But sitting down with them, I think it would definitely help take me to a whole higher level.

Dwight: Yeah. And have you already started to invest in others as far as mentorship, identifying someone that you can mentor, or just giving back?

Gabriel: Oh, yeah. Yeah. So I give back a lot. Just like yesterday alone. I went ahead; one of my soldiers is actually married. So they reached out to me. There are a lot of people that reach out to you, but they consistently reach out to me, and I look at them like, They're young; they just got married. They're like, about 26. And they're looking up to me as a mentor. I'm like, Man, shoot, like, Hey, I feel pretty honored for that.

Dwight: You don't know who is watching.

Gabriel: Yeah. You never know exactly who's watching you. So they said they saw everything from that and how I carried myself at work. And they said that although they're getting out, they definitely want to go ahead and get started. I advised them not to get out right now because, for me, entrepreneurship is great. But still, I think you do need that second income from time to time, especially in the first two to three years. So I showed them everything that I know as far as, like, just a basic class, one-on-one, on what you need to do. They learned how to set up the business first, find out the demand first, and find out the demographics for the area, and they took that advice and were like, just aesthetic about it. Yeah, I definitely want to go ahead and do this. They were way more motivated than when they came in.

Dwight: That's good.

Gabriel: I'm just giving away the free game. Again, as with most people, they charge an arm and a leg. Like the one I have in Hawaii, at first it was a free game. I'll go over to their house, they'll talk, they'll show me different strategies, and then he's like, Yeah, I want a thousand dollars every time.

Dwight: But that's true. I mean, at some point, you have to start charging something for the information that you give, and just like the influencers out there or business coaches, they charge. So you feel like a business coach because you have to coach somebody; it's your time that you're giving. But right now, as you are on your own entrepreneurship journey and learning as you go along for yourself, as you get deeper into learning because you're showing them how to do the paperwork, You're showing them what steps to take and what they have to do, and they're not learning essentially on their own because you're giving them the information. You had to learn it on your own, and as an entrepreneur, sometimes you have to learn certain things on your own. But if you have someone as a coach and as a mentor, at some point you are going to have to start charging for the information because that's your time that you're giving, and in some aspects you can give your time freely if you're volunteering and doing that type of stuff. If you're doing things like the chamber of commerce or different things like that in the community that you get involved in, whether you get involved in the Rotary club, different things in the area, but as far as shaping your business and the experience that you have and sharing that with others, yeah, at some point if you do things like a workshop and things like that, you have to charge because that's your time and people are coming to learn and get the information from you, and they have to be invested because if you don't charge them, they won't be invested as much as if you charge them because now they're putting their money where their mouth is, so to speak.

And so they have to have some form of investment in it because if they don't, then they'll be like, Okay, I'm getting this information and I'm utilizing it. But how often do you have somebody who's willing to take the information that you give them and run with it? But if they feel invested, if they invest something, they have to invest something in it for it to feel like, okay, you're going to be there at, if you're paying a thousand dollars to be there and the meeting starts at eight, I'm going to be there at 8:30, 8:45, but if they don't feel invested in it, then they're going to come at 8:15. Right. So at some point, you're going to have to charge them. So I'm going to finish up here in about a minute or so. How do you balance achieving success in your career with other aspects of your life, such as relationships or personal wellbeing?

Gabriel: And I'd say just strong, because as of right now, that speaks like revelations to my current situation. Right now, I think sometimes relationships are just about your wellbeing. As selfish as it sounds, it sometimes has to take a backseat depending on where you are in your entrepreneurial goals or whatever. The reason being that at critical moments, like setting up a business or setting up just a plan for your next six months, if it's like constant distractions or anything, not distractions, but stuff that typically you invest time to do, Some of the stuff you have to sacrifice, you have to basically sacrifice that time just for that moment so everything can take off. For me, I put myself last sometimes. I know it's bad, but I don't put it to a point where, like, I'm broken down completely. I figure, as far as relationships go, if your family or loved ones don't understand what you're doing, you have to probably sometimes explain it to them, like the step-by-step process or how long it's going to last for us. Everyone will basically have a misconception of what's really going on. They'll look at it differently.

Dwight: Like you're not trying to spend time with them. So how does your spouse feel about that, and how do the kids feel?

Gabriel: It is definitely like, right now it's more of, I guess I don't have this much time, I don't have that much time, but I sit down even with the smallest, the youngest one, and I tell him, Hey, these next six months because I'm moving locations. And what I'm doing right now is something that's never been done, especially self-funded. It's like those people—they don't get off the ground with it. Just the first plan. So I'm moving to a bigger spot that's like a food chain restaurant was in there, so it's that big of a spot to have something in. So I told everyone that the next couple of months were going to be challenging. I would not have a lot of time to go here or there.

Dwight: Between work and business

Gabriel: Exactly.

Dwight: It's difficult, but at least you know that at the end of that goal it's going to pay off dividends, and then you can say, Okay, well, I'm going to take two or three weeks and we are going to go catch up and do this, but here is the plan leading up to that, and you have to stick to that plan and stick to what you say that you're going to do, but yeah, definitely.

Gabriel: So that's exactly what I've been working on and trying to improve on. But sometimes, if your goals don't align or change alignments, you have to evaluate what avenue to go ahead and take. In the long run, once you've invested so much money and time into something and you're like, my coach always used to say, the moment you feel like giving up, the moment where you feel most exhausted, that's your moment of relief that's coming. Like, it's right around the corner; just hold on a little bit longer and squeeze, squeeze. That's one thing. If anything else, don't make it into this book. Pretty much having a mentor from an early age definitely helps because at times where I wouldn't say I feel like quitting because I don't know, it's weird. It scares me sometimes. I don't quit. I just keep on going.

When adversity comes, or any issues or anyone that tried to basically step in, I hear my coach say, It's weird. He's been gone for about, let's say, 12 years, but yet I still hear his voice squeeze. He was just like an epic character with a deep voice. So he never really said French properly. He is like a square-mouthed person. So he was like, "I squeeze French off, squeeze." So I hear that every single time because I used to wrestle in high school, so I hear that every single time when most people would think about quitting. That's when that voice comes in and is like, Okay, well yeah, let's go, let's do this thing, man. Let's make it happen.

Dwight: I hear that. I hear that. You've got to squeeze every ounce of what you have until you lay out flat on the floor. You've got to give it your all until you get to the point where eventually you scale all the businesses that you have, and the potential is there. I'm very proud of you, man, to see the journey that you've taken from the moment that you decided that you wanted to join the military and then just taking off from there. And now that you own multiple businesses, you are on your entrepreneurial journey, which is amazing. I wish your dad was here to see that. And for you to be where you are now, it's amazing to see that and to know that you're building generational wealth. You're creating something not just for yourself but for your family and others down the line. So the last question for you is: in your opinion, is success a destination or a journey, and why?

Gabriel: I'd say success is a journey. As I said before, every time you set a goal and you get close to attaining that goal, a bigger one comes in. As an entrepreneur, at least for me, once you are getting close to accomplishing a goal, you take that little knee moment, you sit down, you look back, and you show a sense of gratitude. Gratitude's a big thing too; if you don't show a sense of gratitude, you'll get nowhere in life you will just feel like if you don't thank God for the simple things, he's not going to reveal the bigger things to you. So that's just one. But the reason I say it's a journey is because it's never-ending. It's just like you always seek betterment. Because if that were the case, once the Neanderthals established fire or got fired, we would've just stayed at that stage and wouldn't have been the advanced civilization we are today.

So I think success is definitely a journey. It basically takes you from one goal to another, then takes you down a path of achieving betterment, and you keep on knocking through that ceiling cap of success or ceiling cap of your goals. Like most people, they try to just block you in, but once you're achieving your goals and moving higher, it definitely puts you in a room where you want to get 10 times bigger. For me, I want to get as successful as possible. At first, I looked at it like regular people, like making a hundred thousand dollars a year was great or would be good. But now it's just like, Why not a million? And so many people talk about that. So it's just like, yeah. It's definitely a journey because it's never-ending.

Dwight: Definitely. Definitely. There are ebbs and flows, and in that entrepreneurial journey, there are ups and downs; there are waves; you go up, you go down; the failures help you grow and build. And you're definitely on that path. So do you see your business being a million-dollar business at the end of FY 24?

Gabriel: Not a million-dollar business yet because the area it's in is a small area, but I see it basically tracked, and for me, like right now on my phone, I have four blocks, and they're all businesses right now. So at first I thought the car rental was going to be the main squeeze, but it's like it's getting so oversaturated. I'm actually thinking about moving out of that realm. But currently, I have the restaurant and lounge. Trucking is a different thing, but the main thing is just the four quads. It is just the four corners. I have the lounge in one area, then car rentals, then trucking, and then the car detailing business. The detailing actually cleans the cars. So it's just like the car rentals all in one. But most outsiders come in sometimes, and they do actually pay for the cleaning because it's like right down the street from other people that do Touro as well.

But I believe once you have four good businesses running at the same time, a million dollars would be no question at all. It's just like [unclear 1:23:47]. So no, the lounge, the restaurant, or the new venture will not be a million-dollar business by the end of the year, but I still know it's coming. My main plan is to branch out in the same way I started over here with just a small hookah lounge. Not really alcohol, but giving the people what they want, and once they have it, that's when you advance after that. So I plan on just replicating it in different military areas and then also in Hawaii, because if anybody knows anything about me, Hawaii is definitely going to be my retirement spot. I don't know when I'll start basically building on that, but still, everything is kind of set up in place for me to move to Hawaii later on in life.

Dwight: Okay. Yeah, definitely. That's good stuff, brother. Yep. So thank you for your time and for sharing. If I have any more side questions or things I just need to clarify as far as dates and things like that, I'll shoot you a text to let you know as I lay this all out for the book, but I appreciate it. Tell my nieces and nephews I said good morning, good afternoon, or whatever time it is now over there. Well, thanks, bro. And I'll let you know when the book is going to drop.

Gabriel: Okay. Alright. Congrats on the book!

Dwight: Thank you. I appreciate it.

Gabriel: Yeah. You've got to mentor me on this process itself. I need someone to write this story.

Dwight: Yes, definitely. That's what I was thinking in my mind when you were talking and stuff. I'm like, Yeah, you've got to write a book from the beginning of your entrepreneurial journey and tie all this information into something and give it to the masses. Give it to them so they can learn and shape their [unclear1:27:33] because people like to see somebody that did it. They like to know somebody who did it and succeeded. And besides going through the failures, which a lot of people don't see, they see the success, the lights, everything that happens, but they don't see the background stuff, the noise that's going on in the background, the construction, the late nights, the early mornings, the sleeping in the new business, that type of stuff. They don't see that type of stuff. So we've got to give them the truth. And I see a lot of that, especially on social media, as well as a lot of people. They tell you one thing, but they don't give you the real story.

Gabriel: The real deal

Dwight: Especially in real estate, you know what I'm saying? It takes capital; it takes leveraging other people's money, but then you can't go get other people's money without having a plan to recoup that money back. You've got to be able—you put that money into the business—to recoup it back because you've got to pay it back at some point. They don't show you a lot of that stuff. And that's what

I don't like about some of those people out there. They put those advertisements out and tell you to join their thing for $97 a month and do this and that. I hate it. The webinars and stuff, and then they offer you all this stuff, but they're just trying to make money for themselves, and they don't tell you the real game. Thank you again. We'll catch up.

Gabriel: Alright, bro.

CHAPTER SEVEN
THE RIPPLE EFFECT OF SUCCESS: HOW SUCCESS GENERATES SUCCESS

"Success is like a stone thrown into a calm lake. Its impact creates ripples that extend far beyond the initial splash, touching the shores of our lives and inspiring others to pursue their own greatness." - Unknown

In this chapter, we will explore the powerful concept of how success generates success. We will delve into the interconnected nature of accomplishments and how success in one area of life can create a ripple effect that propels individuals toward further achievements. By understanding and harnessing this phenomenon, you can unlock your full potential and embark on a continuous growth and success journey.

THE CONFIDENCE CASCADE:

Exploring the Confidence-Success Loop: Success breeds confidence, and confidence breeds further success. Individuals' success validates their efforts and abilities, boosting their self-belief. As their confidence grows, they become more willing to take on challenges, set higher goals, and persist in facing obstacles. For example, imagine someone who completes a marathon. This accomplishment instills a sense of confidence and self-efficacy into other areas of their life, such as their career or personal relationships.

PRACTICAL EXERCISE

"SUCCESS REFLECTION": Reflect on your successes and the confidence those achievements gave you. Write down a list of at least five significant accomplishments you have achieved and the positive impact those successes have had on your confidence and mindset.

SKILL DEVELOPMENT AND TRANSFERABILITY:

The Skill Acquisition Cycle: Success often involves acquiring new skills and knowledge. Each success builds on previous experiences, enabling individuals to develop a versatile skill set that can be applied to different areas of life. For example, someone who excels in project management develops organization, communication, and problem-solving skills. These skills can be transferred to various domains, such as entrepreneurship or community leadership.

Practical Exercise: "Skills Mapping": Identify the skills you have developed through your past successes. Create a visual mind map or list of those skills and brainstorm ways to apply those skills in different areas of your life. Now explore how you can leverage those existing skills to generate further success.

EXPANDING NETWORKS AND COLLABORATIONS

The Power of Connections: Achieving success attracts attention and opens doors to new relationships and opportunities. Successful individuals often surround themselves with a supportive network of mentors, like-minded individuals, and collaborators who provide guidance, support, and valuable resources. For example, a successful entrepreneur may have access to a network of experienced business professionals, investors, or industry experts who can offer advice and open doors to new ventures.

Practical Exercise: "Networking Action Plan": Now, create a networking action plan. Identify key individuals or groups in your field of interest or desired area of success. Research networking events, conferences, or online communities where you can connect with like-minded individuals. Outline specific actions you will take to expand your network and build meaningful relationships within your chosen field.

THE SNOWBALL EFFECT OF RESOURCES:

Accessing Greater Resources: Success often brings increased tangible and intangible resources. Financial success provides individuals with the means to invest in new ventures, pursue further education, or explore personal growth opportunities. Additionally, success can grant individuals access to influential networks, platforms, or resources previously out of reach. For instance, a successful author may gain access to literary agents, publishing opportunities, or speaking engagements.

Practical Exercise: "Resource Optimization": Assess your existing resources and identify how to strategically allocate them for further success. List resources you possess, such as financial resources, skills, knowledge, and networks. Next, brainstorm ways to utilize these resources to propel you forward. For example, invest some of your financial resources in a course or workshop that enhances your skills or knowledge. You could also leverage your existing networks to seek mentorship or collaborative opportunities.

CULTIVATING AN ABUNDANCE MINDSET:

Breaking Through Limiting Beliefs: Success challenges self-imposed limitations and expands belief in what is possible. When individuals experience success, they realize their potential is greater than they thought. They begin to question their self-doubts and break free from the constraints of limiting beliefs. For instance, a successful musician may have doubted their ability to perform on stage, but they overcome their fears and embrace their full potential through practice and successful performances.

Practical Exercise: "Limiting Belief Reframing": Identifying and reframing your limiting beliefs into empowering beliefs. Write down three limiting beliefs that have prevented you from pursuing success in a specific area. Finally, challenge each belief by providing evidence to the contrary and reframe them into empowering beliefs that support your goals and aspirations.

In this chapter, we have explored the remarkable phenomenon of how success generates success. By understanding the interconnected nature of accomplishments, harnessing the confidence cascade, leveraging transferable skills, expanding networks, utilizing resources strategically, and cultivating an abundance mindset. This will take you on a path of continuous growth and achievement. Success begets success, and armed with this knowledge, you, the reader, yes you, can unlock your full potential and create a positive ripple effect throughout your lives.

CHAPTER EIGHT

MY 21-YEAR MILITARY JOURNEY: FINDING SUCCESS THROUGH RECEIPTS OF RESILIENCE

"Success is to be measured not so much by the position that one has reached in life as by the obstacles which he overcame." – Booker T. Washington

Welcome to a chapter that takes you on a personal journey through my life—a life filled with challenges, military service, failed business ventures, and the unbreakable spirit of resilience. This is the story behind "Success Has Receipts," a story that showcases the tangible impact of determination, adaptability, and the relentless pursuit of success.

Introduction: A Military Odyssey

As I share my experiences of navigating a 21-year journey in the military, failed business endeavors, deployments, and constant relocations, I aim to illustrate the powerful concept that "Success Has Receipts." These receipts are not mere papers; they are the battles I've fought, the lessons I've learned, and the victories that have shaped my path.

The Call to Serve: From Enlistment to Leadership

My journey began with the decision to serve my country—a decision that led me through the ranks of the military, from a fresh-faced enlistee to a leader with the responsibility to guide and protect. These early years taught me the receipts of discipline, teamwork, and the art of unwavering commitment. A Commitment not only to my family but to those that had my back and I had theirs.

Facing Defeats: Business Ventures and Bumps in the Road

Beyond my military career, I ventured into the world of business, aiming to translate my leadership skills into entrepreneurial success. However, these ventures weren't without their setbacks. Failed businesses taught me that setbacks weren't roadblocks but receipts of experience, guiding me toward future achievements. So, to you the reader do not give up on your dreams. There is so much more success than failures ahead.

Deployments and Disruptions: Resilience in Action

Deployments took me away from family and familiar surroundings, testing my resilience and adaptability. Navigating different cultures and environments forced me to adapt, discovering the receipt of adaptability and finding strength in the face of uncertainty. Those times really prepared me for now, for today, and I can see now how those uncertain times lead me to where I am today. I will share more of those times in my coming book *"My Stage, My Story."*

From State to State: Embracing Change

The military lifestyle led to frequent relocations, every three years like clockwork. With each move, I discovered the receipt of embracing change, learning to establish new roots, build networks, and find opportunities for growth in the unfamiliar. Do not waste time in the unfamiliar. Become familiar with your surroundings. Meet new people, walk the community you live in and introduce yourself. Some people might not be so welcoming but at least you are breaking free from the uncomfortable and making new friends that may be able to support you on your journey to success.

Triumphs from Tribulations: Turning Setbacks into Receipts

Through my 21-year military journey, I've encountered hardships that, at times, seemed insurmountable. However, these adversities provided the fertile ground for growth. Failed businesses led me to discover new passions, and deployments sharpened my problem-solving skills. Every bump in the road has given me receipts to fuel future successes. By no means did I do it alone. I had God and my family to thank for my success and lifting me back up when I was down.

My journey wasn't without its share of defining moments. These were the instances when I confronted setbacks head-on, transforming them into catalysts for change. Whether it was a failed endeavor, a rejection, or a seemingly insurmountable challenge, each obstacle provided me with valuable receipts that I would later weave into the fabric of my success story.

Continual Learning: The Unseen Receipts

As I moved through each phase of my journey, one constant emerged: the importance of continuous learning. Whether in military strategy, leadership, or entrepreneurship, my success receipts have always included the lessons I've gleaned from every experience and those that I was most fortunate to learn and still learning from.

Inspiring Others: Leading by Example

I share this personal journey not to boast about my experiences but to inspire others to embrace their own journeys. Just as I've found success receipts in my path, so can you. Through determination, resilience, adaptability, and continuous learning, you can navigate your unique journey to measurable success. Amidst the battles, the failures, and the constant change, I discovered that success isn't just a distant dream-it's a collection of hard-earned receipts, forged through determination, resilience, and an unwavering commitment to the journey. Stay the course as you set sail. I look forward to seeing each of you succeed in whatever path you choose.

Conclusion: The Journey Continues

As I reflect on my 21-year military odyssey, filled with deployments, business endeavors, and constant relocations, I'm reminded that success is a journey marked by tangible receipts. The challenges and triumphs, the defeats, and victories—they've all contributed to my success story. And as you've read through this book, and maybe you've highlighted your favorite parts, I encourage you to find the receipts within your journey, paving the way to your own version of success. Thank you and good luck on your journey.

CHAPTER NINE
EMBRACING SUCCESS

"Success is not about the destination, it's about the journey." – Zig Ziglar

Congratulations on reaching the final chapter of this book! Throughout our journey, we have explored various aspects of success, including defining it, developing the right mindset, overcoming obstacles, and executing effective strategies. Now, it's time to reflect on what we've learned and discuss the importance of embracing success wholeheartedly. Know that whenever you embrace something "like a hug", you're making it yours. So, trust it.

RECAP OF KEY POINTS

Let's briefly recap key points discussed in earlier chapters:

- Success is a subjective concept that varies from person to person. It's essential to define what success means to you based on your values, passions, and aspirations.

- The mindset of success is crucial. It involves cultivating a positive attitude, setting clear goals, practicing resilience, and maintaining self-discipline and self-motivation.

- Planning and execution are fundamental to achieving success. Breaking down goals into actionable steps, creating a realistic plan, and consistently taking focused action are essential to the success journey.

- Obstacles and failures are inevitable. Overcoming obstacles requires a growth mindset, problem-solving skills, and resilience. Failure should be viewed as an opportunity for learning, growth, and course correction.

- Embracing success involves celebrating achievements, expressing gratitude, and maintaining a mindset of abundance and positivity. It also requires acknowledging the efforts, sacrifices, and contributions of others along the way.

FINAL THOUGHTS ON PURSUING SUCCESS

Embracing success is about more than achieving goals. It's a mindset shift and a way of living. Here are final thoughts to consider:

- Success is a lifelong journey: Success is not a destination; it's an ongoing process. It's about continually setting new goals, learning, growing, and making a positive impact in your life and the lives of others.

- Success is holistic: True success encompasses various areas of life, including personal growth, relationships, health, and fulfillment. Strive for balance and alignment in all aspects of your life to experience well-rounded and meaningful success.

- Success is unique to you: Avoid comparing your journey to others. Each person's definition of success and the path they take to achieve it will differ. Stay focused on your goals and values and embrace your unique journey.

- Success requires authenticity: Be true to yourself and your values as you pursue success. Authenticity brings fulfillment and attracts opportunities aligned with your true self. Embrace your strengths, passions, and uniqueness as you navigate your path to success.

ENCOURAGEMENT TO EMBRACE SUCCESS

As you conclude this book and continue your journey toward success, I want to offer you some encouragement:

- Believe in yourself: Trust in your abilities and potential. Have faith you have what it takes to achieve your goals. Build confidence by celebrating your wins, big or small, and remind yourself of your progress.

- Embrace continuous growth: Success is not a stagnant state. Embrace a growth mindset and commit to lifelong learning. Seek new knowledge, acquire new skills, and challenge yourself to step outside your comfort zone. Constantly evolve and adapt as you pursue your dreams.

- Surround yourself with support: Cultivate a supportive network of family, friends, mentors, and like-minded individuals who believe in your vision and cheer you on. Seek guidance, collaboration, and encouragement from those who can uplift you on your journey.

- Celebrate milestones: Take the time to celebrate your achievements along the way. Acknowledge your progress, express gratitude for the opportunities you've had, and celebrate the milestones you've reached. Celebrations fuel motivation and provide a sense of accomplishment, reinforcing your commitment to success.

- Practice self-care: Remember to prioritize self-care throughout your journey. Take care of your physical, mental, and emotional well-being. Nurture yourself through activities that recharge and rejuvenate you. Self-care ensures you have the energy and resilience to overcome challenges and pursue success.

TOOLS FOR SUCCESS

To support you in your ongoing pursuit of success, here are practical tools and resources you can utilize:

- Goal-Setting Templates: Utilize goal-setting templates or frameworks to clarify goals, create action plans, and track progress. These templates can help you break down your goals into smaller, actionable steps and visually represent your progress.

- Daily Planner or Journal: Use a daily planner or journal to organize your tasks, set priorities, and reflect on your achievements. This tool helps you stay organized, focused, and accountable for your goals. It also provides a space for self-reflection and gratitude.

- Personal Development Books and Resources: Continuously seek personal development books, podcasts, online courses, and other resources to expand your knowledge, gain new perspectives, and refine your skills. Invest in your personal growth and lifelong learning.

- Networking and Mentorship Opportunities: Engage in networking events, industry conferences, and online communities to connect with like-minded individuals and potential mentors. Building relationships with those who have succeeded in your field can provide valuable guidance, support, and opportunities.

- Visualization and Affirmation Techniques: Harness the power of visualization and affirmations to reinforce your mindset and keep you focused on your goals. Incorporate these practices into your daily routine to enhance your belief in yourself and your ability to achieve success.

- Accountability Systems: Set up accountability systems, such as regular check-ins with an accountability partner, joining a mastermind group, or using goal-tracking apps. These systems help you stay on track, maintain motivation, and take consistent action toward your goals.

Remember, these tools support your journey to success. Experiment with different tools and techniques to find the ones that resonate with you and align with your goals and preferences. Customize them to fit your needs and utilize them consistently to maximize their effectiveness.

Embracing success requires a mindset shift, perseverance, and a commitment to personal growth. As you move forward, trust in yourself, celebrate your progress, and continue to seek tools and resources that support your journey. Embrace the challenges and joys of the success process, knowing you can create the life and achievements you desire. Good luck on your path to success!

Practical Exercise: Creating an Action Plan
Instructions: Write down three actionable steps to embrace success in your life. Consider the insights and principles discussed throughout the book and select actions that resonate with you. Use the Action Plan Worksheet (Example Worksheet 3) to outline your steps, set deadlines, and track your progress.

"SUCCESS HAS RECEIPTS" WORKSHEETS

INSTRUCTIONS:

These worksheets help you develop a roadmap for creating success in your life. Reflect on each question and provide thoughtful responses. Use these worksheets for self-reflection, goal-setting, and personal growth. Answer each question thoughtfully and honestly.

CHAPTER 1: DEFINING SUCCESS AND ITS IMPORTANCE

- How do you define success? Take a moment to reflect and write down your definition.

- Why is success important to you? What drives your desire to achieve success?

- Reflect on the different perceptions of success among individuals. How does your definition of success differ from others?

CHAPTER 2: THE MINDSET OF SUCCESS:

1. SETTING SMART GOALS:

SMART goals are specific, measurable, attainable, relevant, and time-bound. For each area of your life, set one SMART goal representing your vision of success. Write them down below:

Area of Life: _______________________________

SMART Goal: _______________________________

Area of Life: _______________________________

SMART Goal: _______________________________

Area of Life: _______________________________

SMART Goal: _______________________________

2.   IDENTIFYING ACTION STEPS:

For each SMART goal, break it down into actionable steps. Think about what actions you need to take to move closer to your goals. Write down three action steps for each SMART goal:

SMART Goal: _______________________________________

Action Step 1: _____________________________________

Action Step 2: _____________________________________

Action Step 3: _____________________________________

SMART Goal: _______________________________________

Action Step 1: _____________________________________

Action Step 2: _____________________________________

Action Step 3: _____________________________________

SMART Goal: _______________________________________

Action Step 1: _____________________________________

Action Step 2: _____________________________________

Action Step 3: _____________________________________

Overcoming Obstacles:

Anticipate potential obstacles or challenges that may arise along your journey to success. Consider both internal and external factors that could hinder your progress. Answer these questions:

- What obstacles might you encounter?

- How can you proactively address or overcome these obstacles?

- What strategies or resources can you utilize to navigate through challenges?

3. CELEBRATING MILESTONES:

Celebrating your progress and achievements is important for motivation and maintaining momentum. Identify milestones or markers of how you can celebrate. Write down three milestones for each SMART goal:

SMART Goal: _______________________________________

Milestone 1: _______________________________________

Milestone 2: _______________________________________

Milestone 3: _______________________________________

SMART Goal: _______________________________________

Milestone 1: _______________________________________

Milestone 2: _______________________________________

Milestone 3: _______________________________________

SMART Goal: _______________________________________

Milestone 1: _______________________________________

Milestone 2: _______________________________________

Milestone 3: _______________________________________

4. ACCOUNTABILITY:

Consider how you will hold yourself accountable to your goals and action steps. Reflect on these questions:

- How will you track your progress?

- Will you share your goals with someone for added accountability?

- What strategies will you use to stay motivated and focused?

CHAPTER 3: THE POWER OF PLANNING AND EXECUTION:

1. Think about a specific goal you would like to achieve. Write it down below: _______________________________________

2.   Break down your goal into smaller, manageable steps. List three action steps you can take to move closer to your goal:

Action Step 1: ____

Action Step 2: ____

Action Step 3: ____

3.   How will you incorporate consistency into your journey? What strategies will you use to stay on track with your action steps?

CHAPTER 4: OVERCOMING OBSTACLES AND FAILURE

1.   Identify a recent setback or failure you have experienced. Reflect on what you learned from it and how it has contributed to your growth.

2.   How do you typically deal with self-doubt and negative self-talk? What strategies can you employ to overcome these challenges?

3.   Share one valuable lesson you have learned from a failure or setback. How has it helped you become more resilient and determined?

CHAPTER 5: EMBRACING SUCCESS

1.   Recap the key points from the previous chapters that resonated most with you. Write them down and reflect on their significance in your journey toward success.

2.   Write down your final thoughts on pursuing success. How has your perspective on success evolved throughout the book?

3.   Share an encouraging message to yourself and to others striving for success.

CHAPTER 6: THE RIPPLE EFFECT OF SUCCESS: HOW SUCCESS GENERATES SUCCESS

1.   Reflect on past successes you have achieved. How have these successes positively impacted other areas of your life or inspired others around you?

2.   How can you actively seek opportunities to support and uplift others in their pursuit of success? Write down three ways you can contribute to the success of others.

3.   Consider how the concept of success generating success applies to your life. How can you harness this principle to create a positive ripple effect in your journey toward success?

CHAPTER 7: UNLOCKING THE POWER OF SUCCESS

Instructions:

This worksheet helps you explore how success generates success and apply it to your life. Reflect on each question and provide thoughtful responses. Be honest with yourself and use this worksheet for self-discovery and personal growth.

1.   REFLECTING ON PAST SUCCESSES:

 Think about three significant successes you have achieved in your life. These could be personal, academic, professional, or any other area of your life. Write them down below:

1. ____

2. ____

3. ____

For each success, answer these questions:

- How did this success make you feel? What positive emotions did it bring?

- Did this success boost your confidence? In what ways?

- Did this success open doors to new opportunities or relationships? Explain.

2.   THE CONFIDENCE CASCADE:

Consider a recent success you have experienced or one that stands out to you. It could be big or small. Write it down below:

____

Reflect on these questions:

- How did this success impact your confidence? Did it encourage you to take on new challenges?

- Did this success inspire you to set higher goals or aim for more significant achievements?

- How has this success influenced your mindset and belief in your abilities?

Practical Action Step: Identify one new challenge or goal you feel motivated to pursue because of your recent success. Write it down and outline three action steps you can take to move closer to that goal.

New Challenge/Goal: _________________________________

Action Steps:

1. ____

2. ____

3. ____

3.	SKILL DEVELOPMENT AND TRANSFERABILITY:

Think about a skill or knowledge area in which you have achieved success. It could be a professional skill, a hobby, or an area of expertise. Write it down below:

____

Reflect on these questions:
- How did you develop this skill? What steps did you take to become successful?
- How can you transfer this skill or knowledge to other areas of your life?
- How can this skill contribute to your future successes and goals?

Practical Action Step: Identify one area of your life where you can apply or develop this skill further. Write it down and outline three action steps you can take to enhance your skills.

Area of Application/Development: _____________________________

Action Steps:
1. ____
2. ____
3. ____

4.	EXPANDING NETWORKS AND COLLABORATIONS:

Think about individuals or groups who have supported you in your successes. They could be mentors, colleagues, friends, or anyone who has played a role in your achievements. Write down their names and how they have contributed to your success:

1. ____
Contribution: _______________________________________
2. ____
Contribution: _______________________________________
3. ____
Contribution: _______________________________________

Reflect on these questions:
- How have these individuals or groups positively influenced your path to success?
- How can you further expand your network and seek collaborative opportunities?
- In what ways can you contribute to the success of others and create a supportive ecosystem?

Practical Action Step: Reach out to one person from your network and express your gratitude for their support. Additionally, identify one new networking opportunity or collaborative project you can explore. Write them down below:

Person to Express Gratitude: _______________________________________

Networking Opportunity/Collaborative Project: _______________________

Action Steps: _______________________________________

____

4. CULTIVATING AN ABUNDANCE MINDSET:

Consider a limiting belief you have held about your abilities or potential for success. Write it down below:

Reflect on these questions:

- How has this limiting belief held you back from pursuing success?

- What evidence or experiences can you gather to challenge this belief?

- How can you reframe this belief into an empowering belief that supports your growth and success?

Practical Action Step: Take one small action that defies your limiting belief and aligns with your empowering belief. Write it down and commit to taking that action within the next week.

Empowering Belief: ____

Action Step: ____

CHAPTER 9: SUSTAINING SUCCESS

1.   Assessing Your Current Level of Success:

Rate your current level of success on a scale of 1-10 (1 being low and 10 being high) in these areas:

- Career/Professional Success:

- Personal Growth and Development:

- Health and Well-being:

- Relationships (Family, Friends, Romantic):

- Financial Stability:

2.   Recognizing Factors that Contributed to Your Success:

Reflect on the key factors or habits that have contributed to your current success. Write down at least three factors for each area of success you rated highly:

Career/Professional Success:

Personal Growth and Development:

Health and Well-being:

Relationships:

Financial Stability:

3.   Identifying Areas for Continued Growth:

Evaluate the areas where you feel there is room for improvement or further growth. Write down one specific action you can take for each area to sustain and enhance your success:

Career/Professional Success:
Action Step: ____
Personal Growth and Development:
Action Step: ____
____

Health and Well-being:
Action Step: ____
____

Relationships:
Action Step: ____
Financial Stability: ______________________________________
Action Step: ____

4.	Maintaining Balance and Well-being:

Reflect on how you prioritize your well-being and maintain balance in your life. Answer these questions:

- How do you manage stress and prevent burnout?

- What self-care practices do you engage in regularly?

- How do you ensure that you have a healthy work-life balance?

5.	Celebrating and Rewarding Success:

Think about how you acknowledge and celebrate your successes. Answer these questions:

- How do you celebrate your achievements, both big and small?

- What rewards or incentives do you give yourself when you reach milestones?

- How can you incorporate more celebration and reward into your success journey?

CONCLUSION

Congratulations on completing the worksheets! By exploring these concepts and engaging in practical exercises, you have taken a significant step toward unlocking your full potential. Review your responses regularly and act on the outlined steps to propel your success forward.

Note: These worksheets are a tool for self-reflection and personal growth. Revisit it whenever you need a reminder of the power of success and its ability to generate further success.

Last, engaging in these exercises, you can explore your beliefs and perspectives on success. It encourages self-reflection and helps clarify your definition of success, which may differ from societal or external expectations. These exercises will help you connect with your values and aspirations, enabling you to pursue a path of success that feels fulfilling and meaningful in your journey. Good luck!!

ABOUT THE AUTHOR

Dwight D. Fleary is a new dynamic and influential author, with Pen and Parchment Publishing. With a passion for personal development and achieving one's full potential, Dwight's writing resonates deeply with readers seeking inspiration and guidance on their journey to success.

In "Success Has Receipts," Dwight shares his insights and strategies, drawing from his own and the experiences of those who became successful through resilience and purpose. Through his engaging prose, he empowers readers to unlock their potential, overcome obstacles, and create a life of purpose and fulfillment.

Dwight's own journey to success is an inspiring tale of determination and resilience. From humble beginnings, he tirelessly pursued his dreams, learning valuable lessons along the way. Born in Brooklyn, NY with West-Indian roots, Dwight has a bachelor's degree in music technology and a master's in health-care administration. With over 21 years of military service, his unwavering belief in the power of self-belief, goal-setting, and constant action has propelled him to remarkable achievements, and now he shares his wisdom with others.

With a unique ability to distill complex concepts into practical steps, Dwight provides readers with a roadmap with for personal and professional growth. His writing delves into topics such as mindset, productivity, effective communication, and building lasting relationships-all crucial elements for achieving success in today's rapidly evolving world.

Dwight Fleary's writing is more than just motivational-it is a call to action. Through his book, he empowers readers to embrace their individuality, unleash their true potential, and create the life they always envisioned. His authentic and relatable approach resonates with readers from all walks of life, making "Success Has Receipts" a must-read for those hungry for personal and professional transformation.

Join Dwight Fleary on a transformative journey as he imparts invaluable wisdom and equips readers with the tools, they need to manifest their dreams. Prepare to be inspired, motivated, and armed with actionable steps necessary to turn aspirations into tangible achievements. He is currently working on his second book for print, "Receipts of Resilience: Navigating Challenges on the Path to Success."

Success Has Receipts Questionnaire: Where Do You Stand?

1. Determination: On a scale of 1 to 10, how determined are you to achieve your goals? (1 being low, 10 being extremely determined)
2. Resilience: Rate your ability to bounce back from setbacks. How well do you handle challenges? (1 to 10)
3. Adaptability: How comfortable are you with change and adapting to new situations? (1 to 10)
4. Continuous Learning: How often do you actively seek new knowledge or skills to improve yourself? (1 to 10)
5. Goal Setting: How skilled are you at setting clear, measurable goals for yourself? (1 to 10)
6. Time Management: Rate your ability to effectively manage your time and prioritize tasks. (1 to 10)
7. Networking: How strong is your network of connections and supporters? (1 to 10)
8. Problem Solving: How confident are you in your ability to find solutions to challenges? (1 to 10)
9. Celebrating Wins: How often do you take time to acknowledge and celebrate your achievements? (1 to 10)
10. Support System: How well do you surround yourself with people who encourage and inspire you? (1 to 10)

Scoring:

Add up your scores for each question to get your total score out of 100. This will help you assess where you stand in terms of the "receipts" that lead to success.

Interpretation:

- 0-40: There's room for improvement. Focus on building the foundational "receipts" of success.
- 41-70: You're on the right track, but there's still potential for growth. Keep refining your "receipts."
- 71-100: Congratulations! You're well-equipped with the "receipts" for success. Continue to refine and inspire others.

Once you take the questionnaire please reflect on your scores.

NOTES

1.   "The Alchemist" by Paulo Coelho. (1988).
This renowned novel explores the theme of personal destiny and the importance of following one's dreams. It emphasizes the transformative power of pursuing one's goals and the lessons learned along the journey.

2.   "Think and Grow Rich" by Napoleon Hill. (1937).
This classic self-help book delves into the mindset and principles of success. It outlines strategies for developing a success-oriented mindset, setting goals, and overcoming obstacles on the path to achievement.

3.   "Man's Search for Meaning" by Viktor E. Frankl. (1946).
This powerful memoir explores the author's experiences in Nazi concentration camps during World War II. It delves into the search for meaning in life and the resilience of the human spirit, providing profound insights into finding purpose and success amidst adversity.

4.   "The 7 Habits of Highly Effective People" by Stephen R. Covey. (1989).
This influential self-help book presents a holistic approach to personal and professional effectiveness. It outlines seven key habits that can empower individuals to achieve success, focusing on principles such as proactive behavior, prioritization, and synergy.

5.   "Mindset: The New Psychology of Success" by Carol S. Dweck. (2006).
This book explores the concept of mindset and its impact on personal

and professional success. It distinguishes between a fixed mindset, which limits growth and potential, and a growth mindset, which embraces challenges and believes in the ability to develop and improve.

6.   "Outliers: The Story of Success" by Malcolm Gladwell. (2008). In this thought-provoking book, Gladwell examines the factors that contribute to exceptional success. He explores the idea that success is often a result of a combination of factors, including opportunity, cultural background, and dedicated practice.